AMAZING INVENTIONS
SNEAKERS
A GRAPHIC HISTORY

BLAKE HOENA

ILLUSTRATED BY **CEEJ ROWLAND**

Graphic Universe™ • Minneapolis

Graphic Universe™
An imprint of Lerner Publishing Group, Inc.
241 First Avenue North
Minneapolis, MN 55401 USA

For reading levels and more information, look up this title at www.lernerbooks.com.

Main body text set in CCHedgeBackwards 7/9
Typeface provided by Comicraft.

Library of Congress Cataloging-in-Publication Data

Names: Hoena, B. A. writer. | Rowland, Ceej, illustrator.
Title: Sneakers : a graphic history / written by Blake Hoena ; illustrated by Ceej Rowland.
Description: Minneapolis : Graphic Universe, [2021] | Series: Amazing inventions | Includes bibliographical references and index. | Audience: Ages 8–12 | Audience: Grades 4–6 | Summary: "Sneakers grew out of efforts to make more durable, more comfortable shoes-and became a major link between sports and fashion. Their rising popularity led to celebrity endorsements, big-name brands, and ongoing technological breakthroughs"— Provided by publisher.
Identifiers: LCCN 2020006425 (print) | LCCN 2020006426 (ebook) | ISBN 9781541581487 (library binding) | ISBN 9781728417462 (ebook)
Subjects: LCSH: Sneakers—Comic books, strips, etc.—Juvenile literature. | Graphic novels.
Classification: LCC TS1017 .H64 2021 (print) | LCC TS1017 (ebook) | DDC 685.31—dc23

LC record available at https://lccn.loc.gov/2020006425
LC ebook record available at https://lccn.loc.gov/2020006426

Manufactured in the United States of America
1 - 47331 - 47958 - 2/5/2021

TABLE OF CONTENTS

CHAPTER 1
RUBBER REVOLUTION

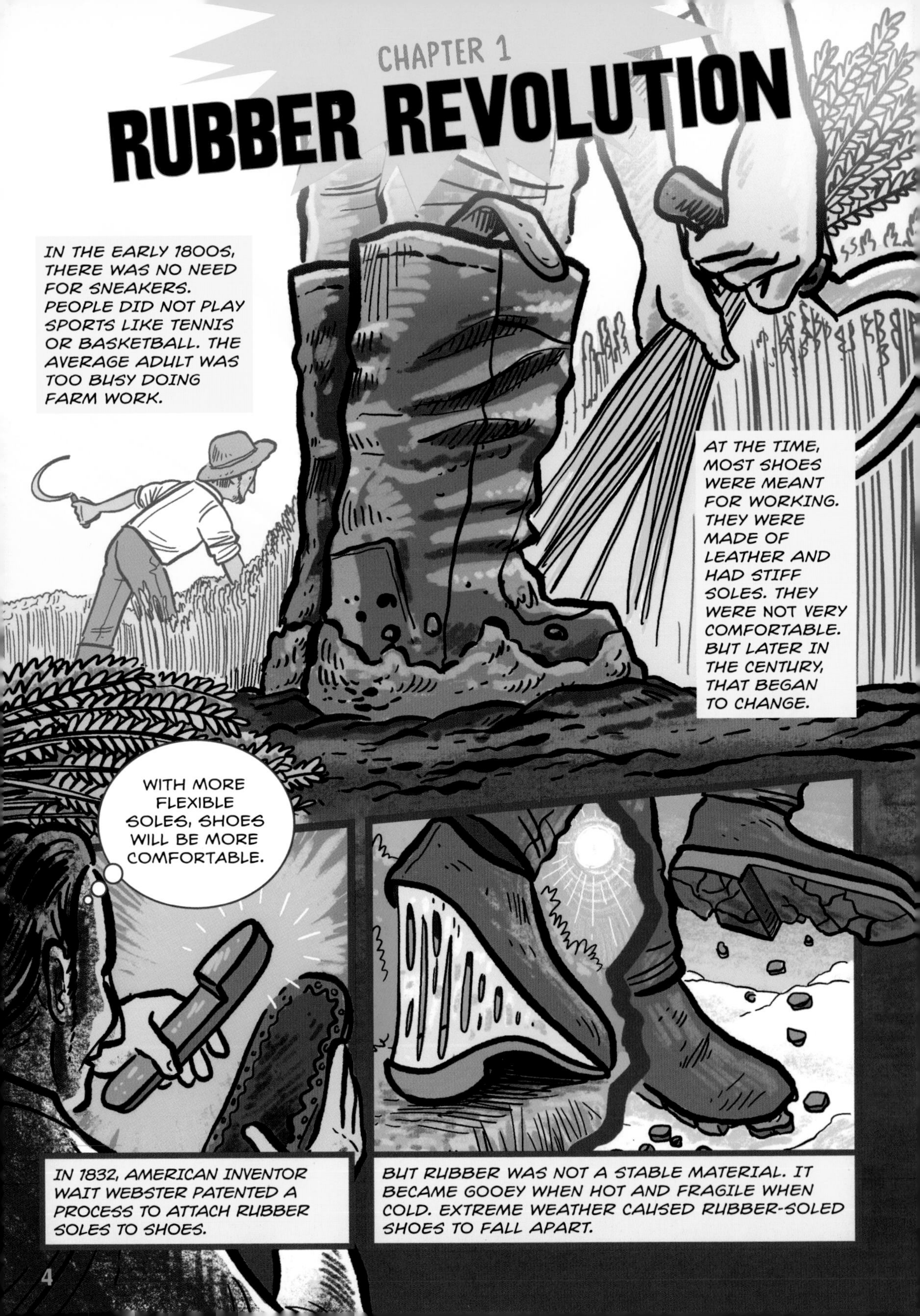
IN THE EARLY 1800S, THERE WAS NO NEED FOR SNEAKERS. PEOPLE DID NOT PLAY SPORTS LIKE TENNIS OR BASKETBALL. THE AVERAGE ADULT WAS TOO BUSY DOING FARM WORK.
AT THE TIME, MOST SHOES WERE MEANT FOR WORKING. THEY WERE MADE OF LEATHER AND HAD STIFF SOLES. THEY WERE NOT VERY COMFORTABLE. BUT LATER IN THE CENTURY, THAT BEGAN TO CHANGE.
WITH MORE FLEXIBLE SOLES, SHOES WILL BE MORE COMFORTABLE.
IN 1832, AMERICAN INVENTOR WAIT WEBSTER PATENTED A PROCESS TO ATTACH RUBBER SOLES TO SHOES.
BUT RUBBER WAS NOT A STABLE MATERIAL. IT BECAME GOOEY WHEN HOT AND FRAGILE WHEN COLD. EXTREME WEATHER CAUSED RUBBER-SOLED SHOES TO FALL APART.

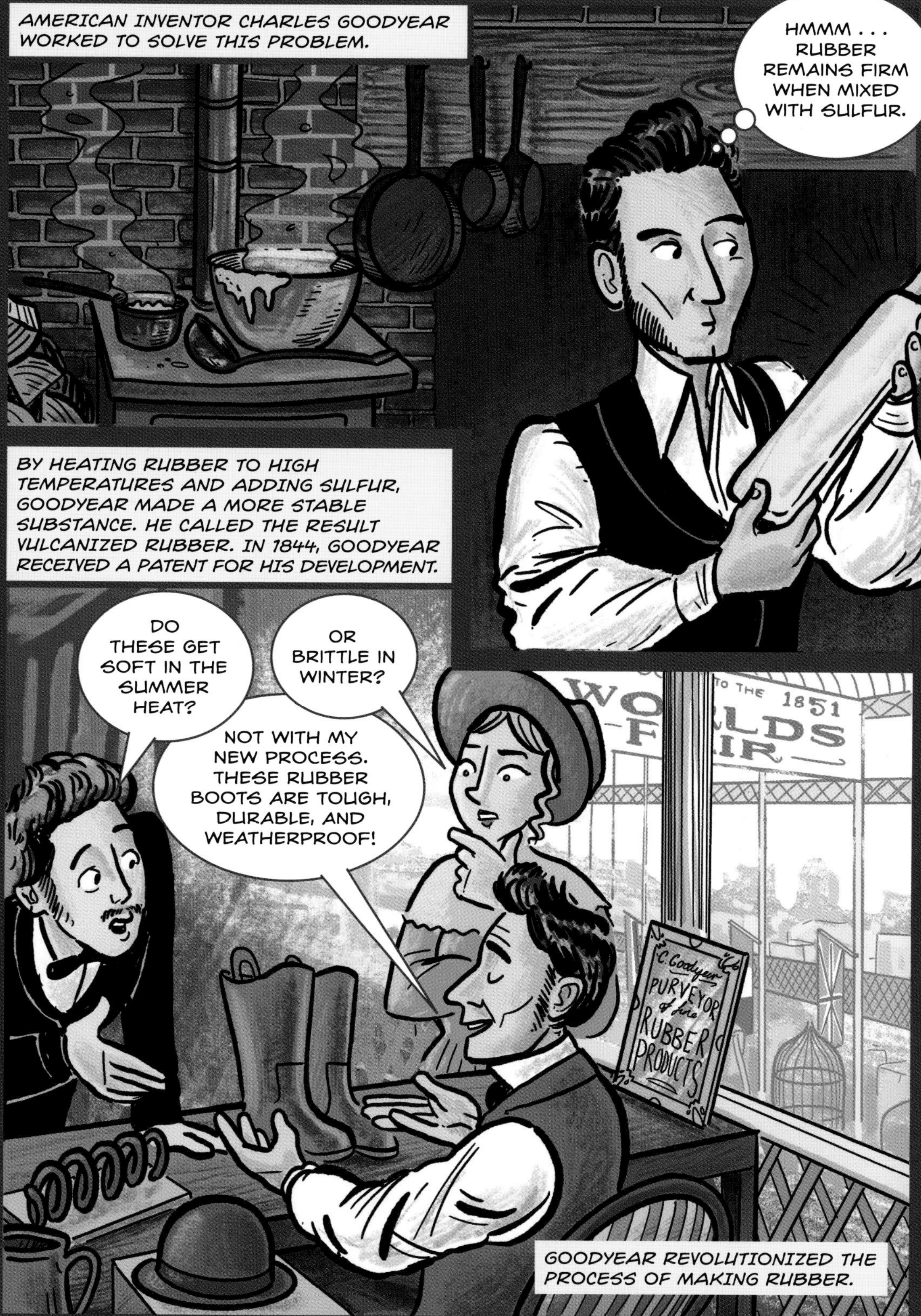
AMERICAN INVENTOR CHARLES GOODYEAR WORKED TO SOLVE THIS PROBLEM.
HMMM . . . RUBBER REMAINS FIRM WHEN MIXED WITH SULFUR.
BY HEATING RUBBER TO HIGH TEMPERATURES AND ADDING SULFUR, GOODYEAR MADE A MORE STABLE SUBSTANCE. HE CALLED THE RESULT VULCANIZED RUBBER. IN 1844, GOODYEAR RECEIVED A PATENT FOR HIS DEVELOPMENT.
DO THESE GET SOFT IN THE SUMMER HEAT?
OR BRITTLE IN WINTER?
NOT WITH MY NEW PROCESS. THESE RUBBER BOOTS ARE TOUGH, DURABLE, AND WEATHERPROOF!
TO THE 1851 WORLDS FAIR
C. Goodyear PURVEYOR of fine RUBBER PRODUCTS
GOODYEAR REVOLUTIONIZED THE PROCESS OF MAKING RUBBER.

AS GOODYEAR WAS WORKING ON HIS INVENTION, THE INDUSTRIAL REVOLUTION WAS CHANGING PEOPLE'S LIVES. MANY MOVED FROM THE COUNTRY TO WORK IN OR OVERSEE URBAN FACTORIES. FOR SOME FORTUNATE, WEALTHY PEOPLE, THIS CHANGE MEANT MORE LEISURE TIME. SPORTS SUCH AS CROQUET BECAME POPULAR.

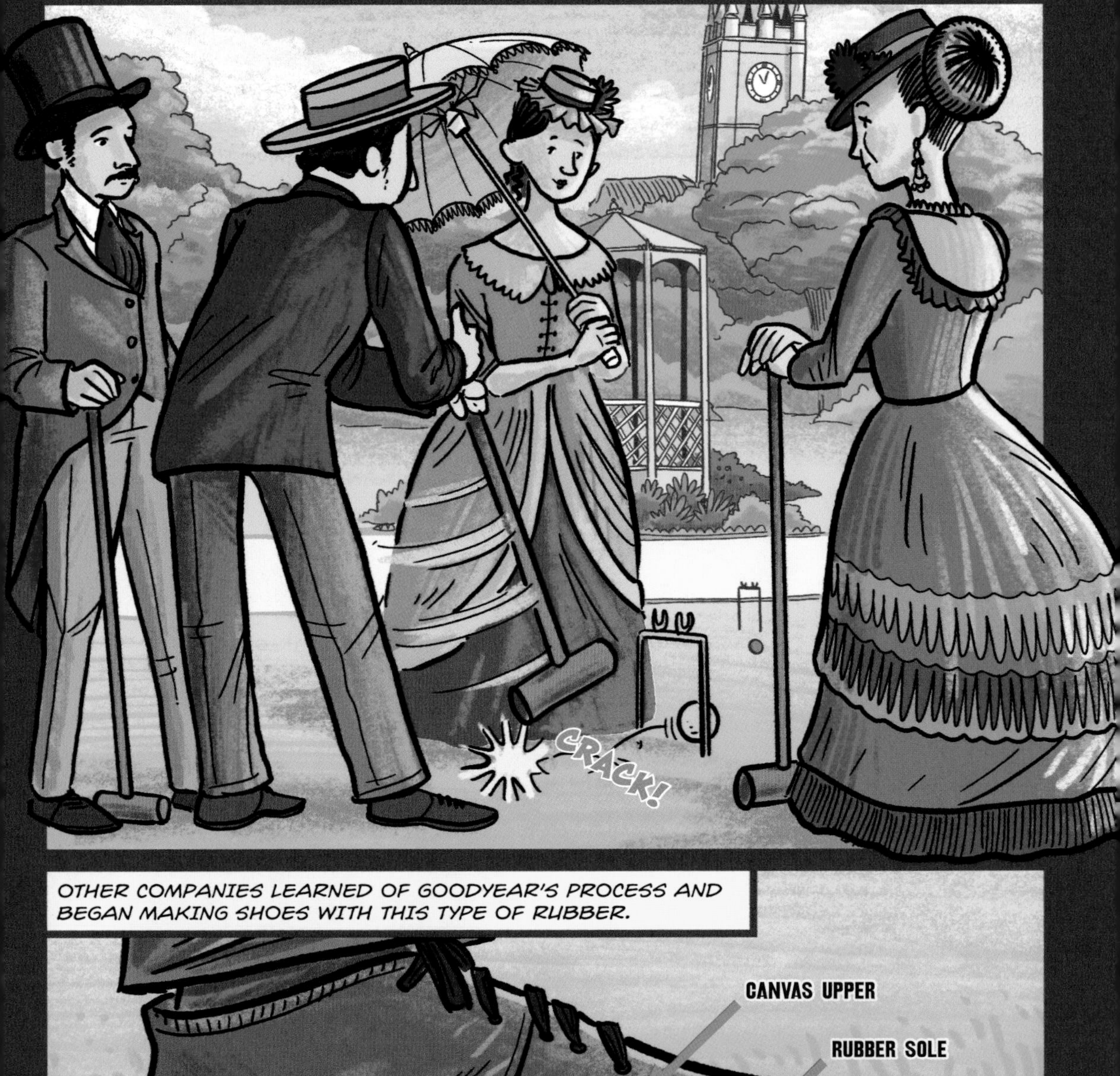
CRACK!

OTHER COMPANIES LEARNED OF GOODYEAR'S PROCESS AND BEGAN MAKING SHOES WITH THIS TYPE OF RUBBER.

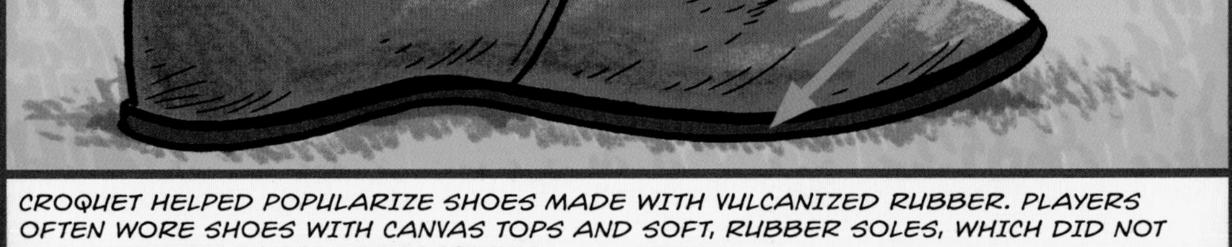
CANVAS UPPER
RUBBER SOLE

CROQUET HELPED POPULARIZE SHOES MADE WITH VULCANIZED RUBBER. PLAYERS OFTEN WORE SHOES WITH CANVAS TOPS AND SOFT, RUBBER SOLES, WHICH DID NOT LEAVE INDENTS IN THE GRASS COURTS.

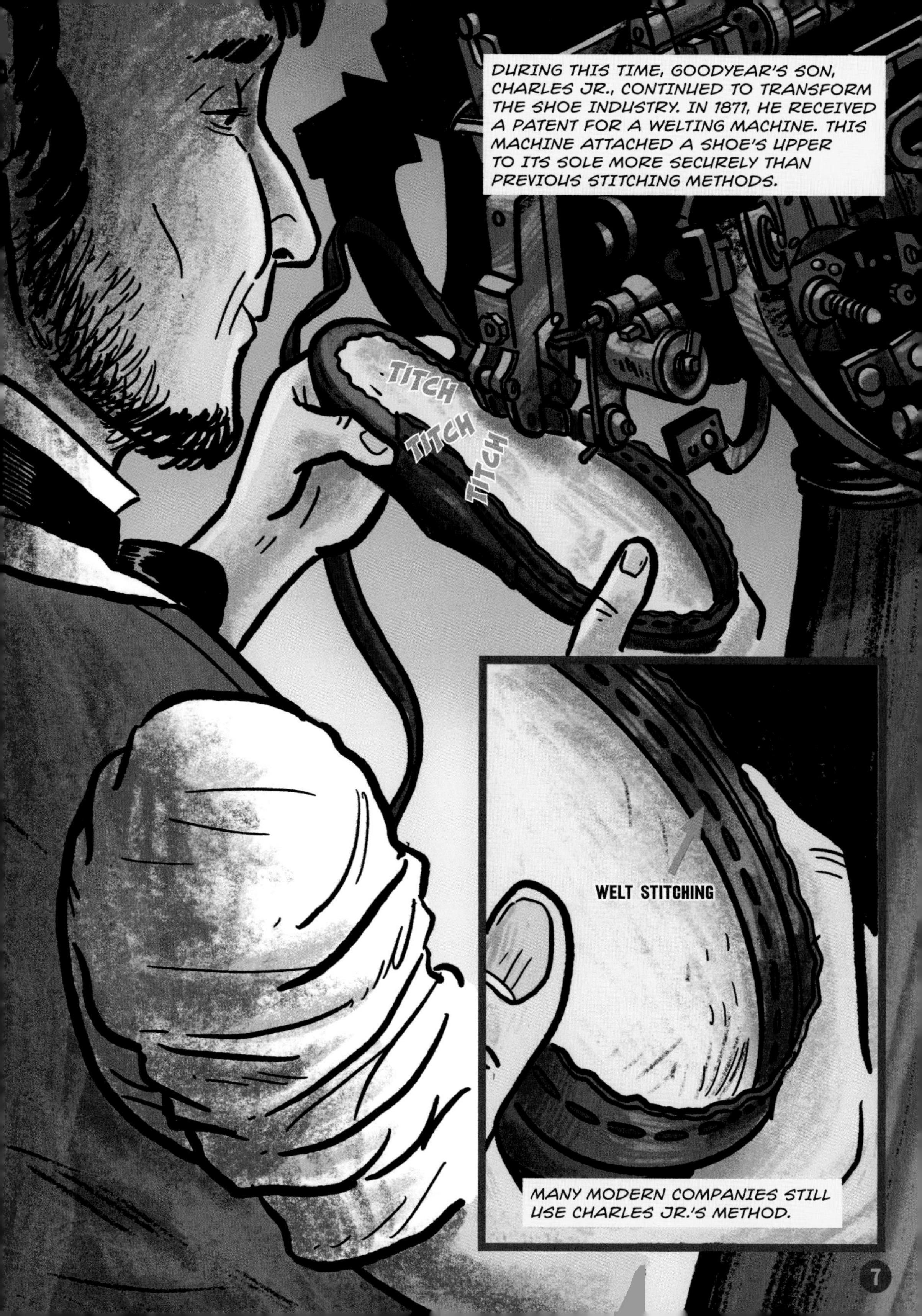
DURING THIS TIME, GOODYEAR'S SON, CHARLES JR., CONTINUED TO TRANSFORM THE SHOE INDUSTRY. IN 1871, HE RECEIVED A PATENT FOR A WELTING MACHINE. THIS MACHINE ATTACHED A SHOE'S UPPER TO ITS SOLE MORE SECURELY THAN PREVIOUS STITCHING METHODS.
TITCH
TITCH
TITCH
WELT STITCHING
MANY MODERN COMPANIES STILL USE CHARLES JR.'S METHOD.

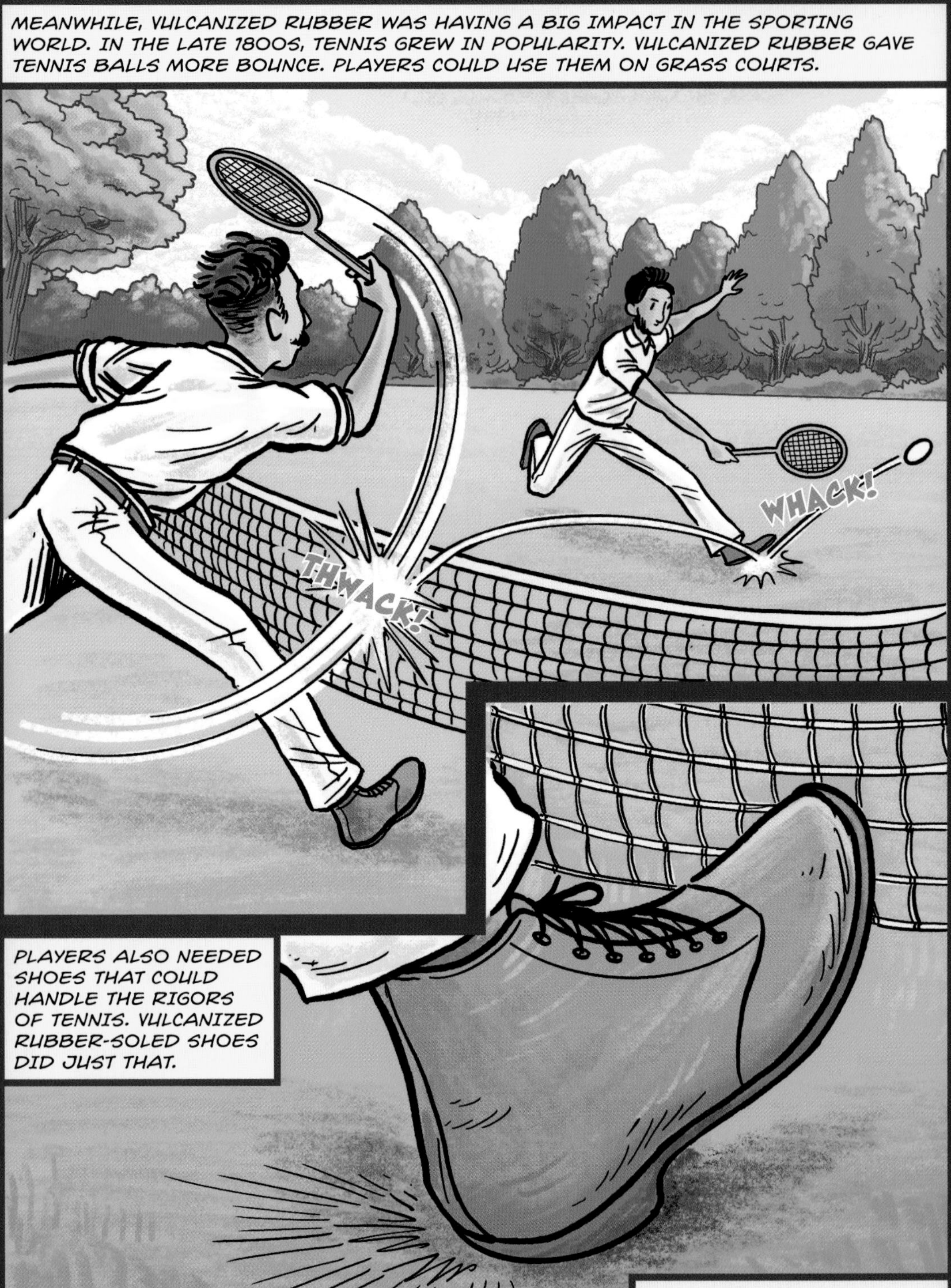
MEANWHILE, VULCANIZED RUBBER WAS HAVING A BIG IMPACT IN THE SPORTING WORLD. IN THE LATE 1800S, TENNIS GREW IN POPULARITY. VULCANIZED RUBBER GAVE TENNIS BALLS MORE BOUNCE. PLAYERS COULD USE THEM ON GRASS COURTS.
THWACK!
WHACK!
PLAYERS ALSO NEEDED SHOES THAT COULD HANDLE THE RIGORS OF TENNIS. VULCANIZED RUBBER-SOLED SHOES DID JUST THAT.
AS TENNIS SPREAD, SO DID THE SPORT'S FOOTWEAR. IT SOON BECAME KNOWN AS THE TENNIS SHOE.

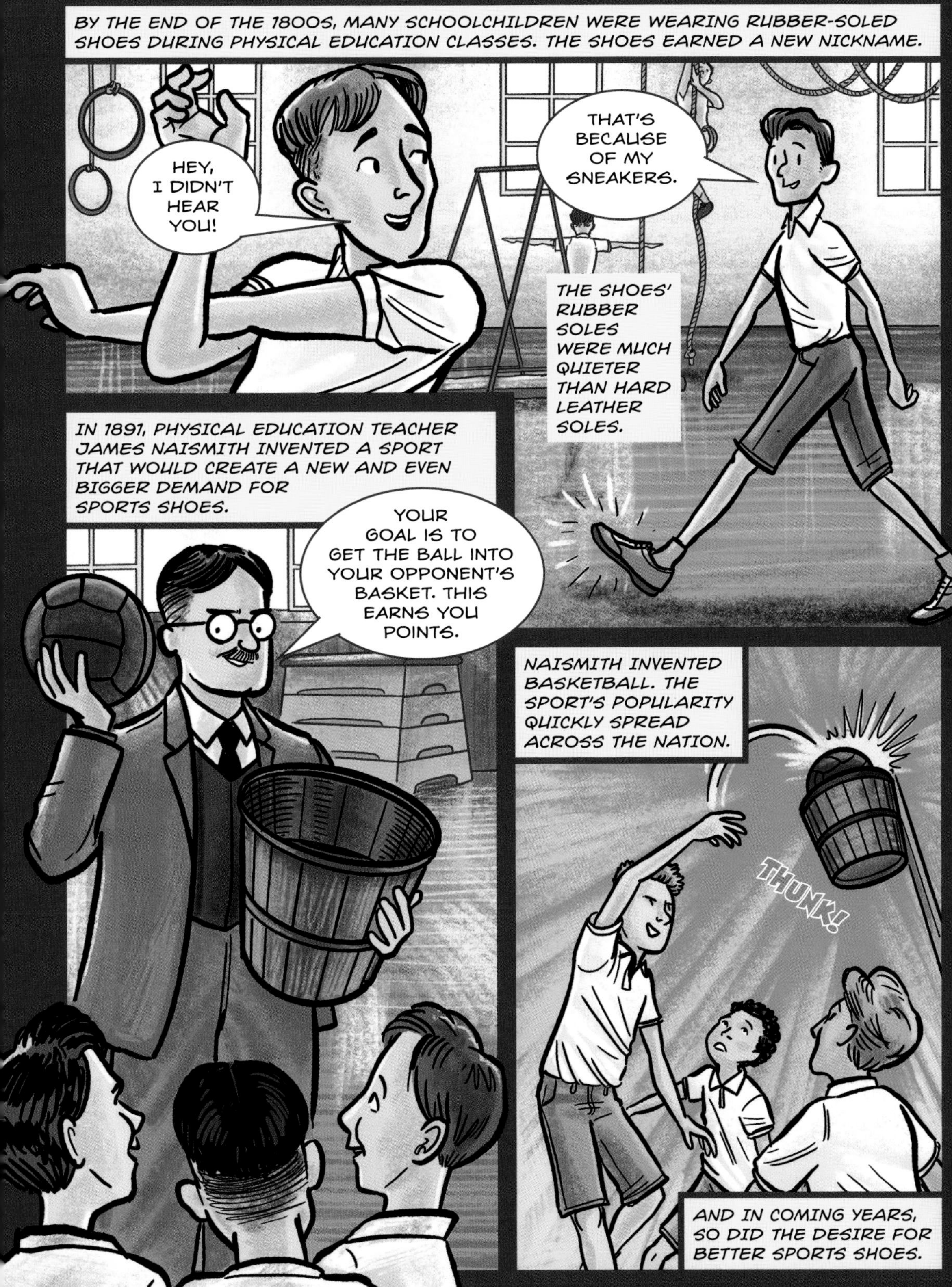
BY THE END OF THE 1800S, MANY SCHOOLCHILDREN WERE WEARING RUBBER-SOLED SHOES DURING PHYSICAL EDUCATION CLASSES. THE SHOES EARNED A NEW NICKNAME.
HEY, I DIDN'T HEAR YOU!
THAT'S BECAUSE OF MY SNEAKERS.
THE SHOES' RUBBER SOLES WERE MUCH QUIETER THAN HARD LEATHER SOLES.
IN 1891, PHYSICAL EDUCATION TEACHER JAMES NAISMITH INVENTED A SPORT THAT WOULD CREATE A NEW AND EVEN BIGGER DEMAND FOR SPORTS SHOES.
YOUR GOAL IS TO GET THE BALL INTO YOUR OPPONENT'S BASKET. THIS EARNS YOU POINTS.
NAISMITH INVENTED BASKETBALL. THE SPORT'S POPULARITY QUICKLY SPREAD ACROSS THE NATION.
THUNK!
AND IN COMING YEARS, SO DID THE DESIRE FOR BETTER SPORTS SHOES.

CHAPTER 2
BASKETBALL BOOM

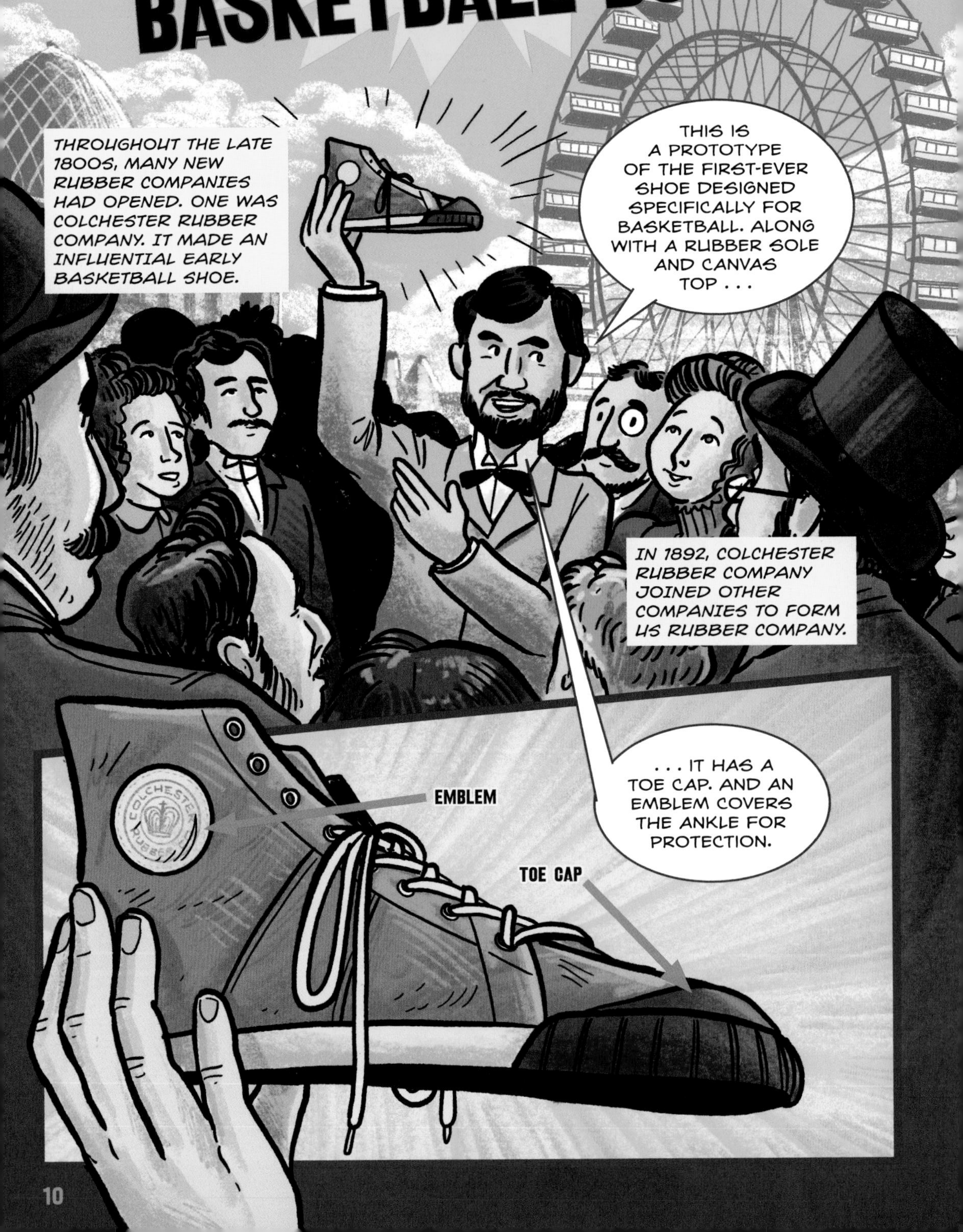

THROUGHOUT THE LATE 1800S, MANY NEW RUBBER COMPANIES HAD OPENED. ONE WAS COLCHESTER RUBBER COMPANY. IT MADE AN INFLUENTIAL EARLY BASKETBALL SHOE.
THIS IS A PROTOTYPE OF THE FIRST-EVER SHOE DESIGNED SPECIFICALLY FOR BASKETBALL. ALONG WITH A RUBBER SOLE AND CANVAS TOP . . .
IN 1892, COLCHESTER RUBBER COMPANY JOINED OTHER COMPANIES TO FORM US RUBBER COMPANY.
. . . IT HAS A TOE CAP. AND AN EMBLEM COVERS THE ANKLE FOR PROTECTION.
EMBLEM
TOE CAP

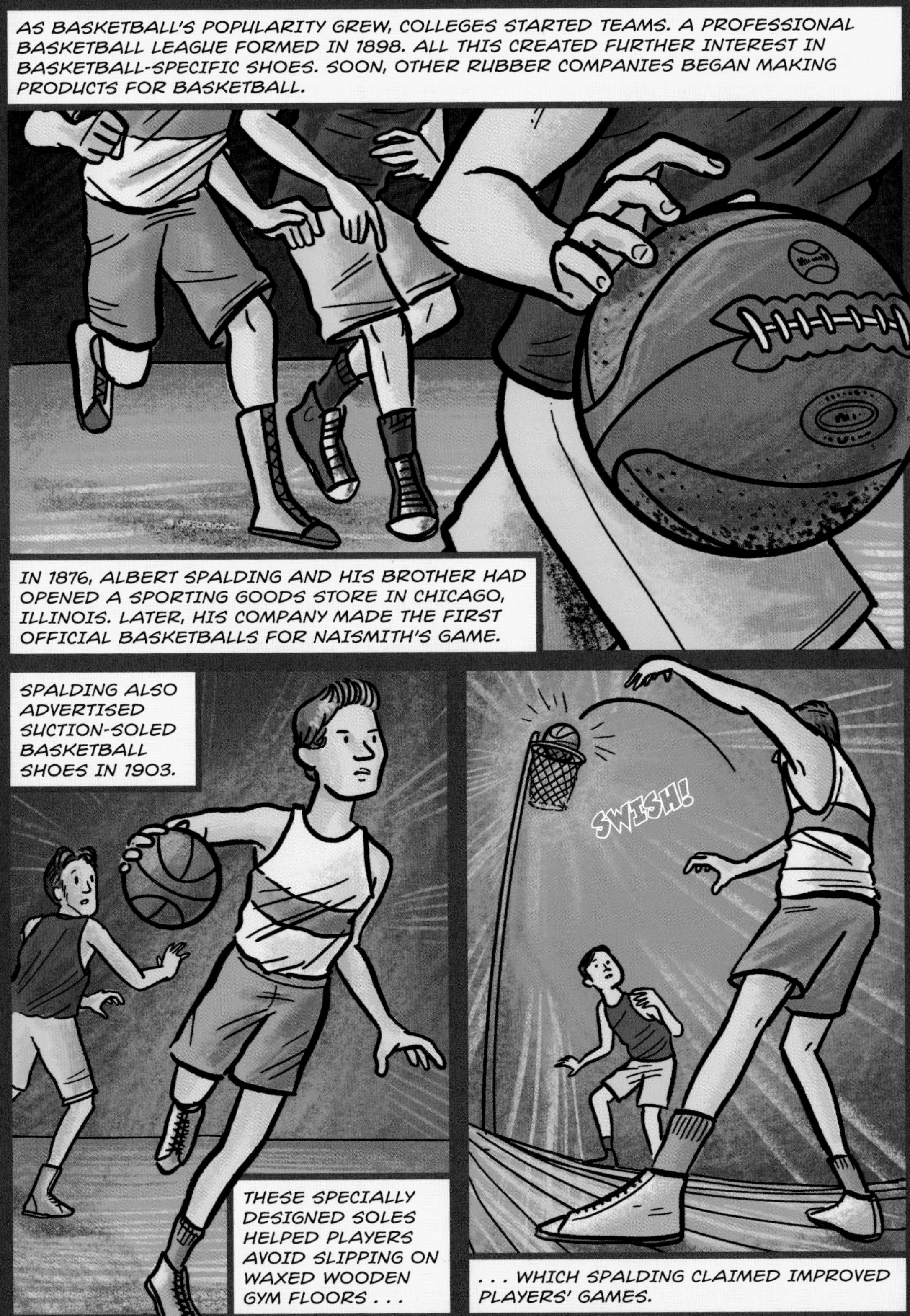
AS BASKETBALL'S POPULARITY GREW, COLLEGES STARTED TEAMS. A PROFESSIONAL BASKETBALL LEAGUE FORMED IN 1898. ALL THIS CREATED FURTHER INTEREST IN BASKETBALL-SPECIFIC SHOES. SOON, OTHER RUBBER COMPANIES BEGAN MAKING PRODUCTS FOR BASKETBALL.
IN 1876, ALBERT SPALDING AND HIS BROTHER HAD OPENED A SPORTING GOODS STORE IN CHICAGO, ILLINOIS. LATER, HIS COMPANY MADE THE FIRST OFFICIAL BASKETBALLS FOR NAISMITH'S GAME.
SPALDING ALSO ADVERTISED SUCTION-SOLED BASKETBALL SHOES IN 1903.
THESE SPECIALLY DESIGNED SOLES HELPED PLAYERS AVOID SLIPPING ON WAXED WOODEN GYM FLOORS . . .
SWISH!
. . . WHICH SPALDING CLAIMED IMPROVED PLAYERS' GAMES.

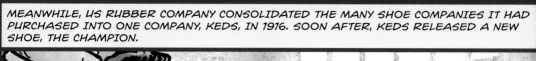

MEANWHILE, US RUBBER COMPANY CONSOLIDATED THE MANY SHOE COMPANIES IT HAD PURCHASED INTO ONE COMPANY, KEDS, IN 1916. SOON AFTER, KEDS RELEASED A NEW SHOE, THE CHAMPION.

WHILE THE TERM "SNEAKER" HAD ALREADY BEEN COINED, IT CAME INTO MORE COMMON USAGE AROUND THIS TIME.

WEARING SNEAKERS FOR EVERYDAY ACTIVITIES ALSO BECAME MORE COMMON. KEDS ADVERTISED THAT ITS SNEAKERS WERE NOT JUST FOR SPORTS BUT FOR ANYONE WANTING A COMFORTABLE AND STYLISH SHOE. ON THE HEELS OF THE CHAMPION'S RELEASE, ANOTHER COMPANY WOULD BRING SNEAKERS' POPULARITY TO A NEW LEVEL . . .

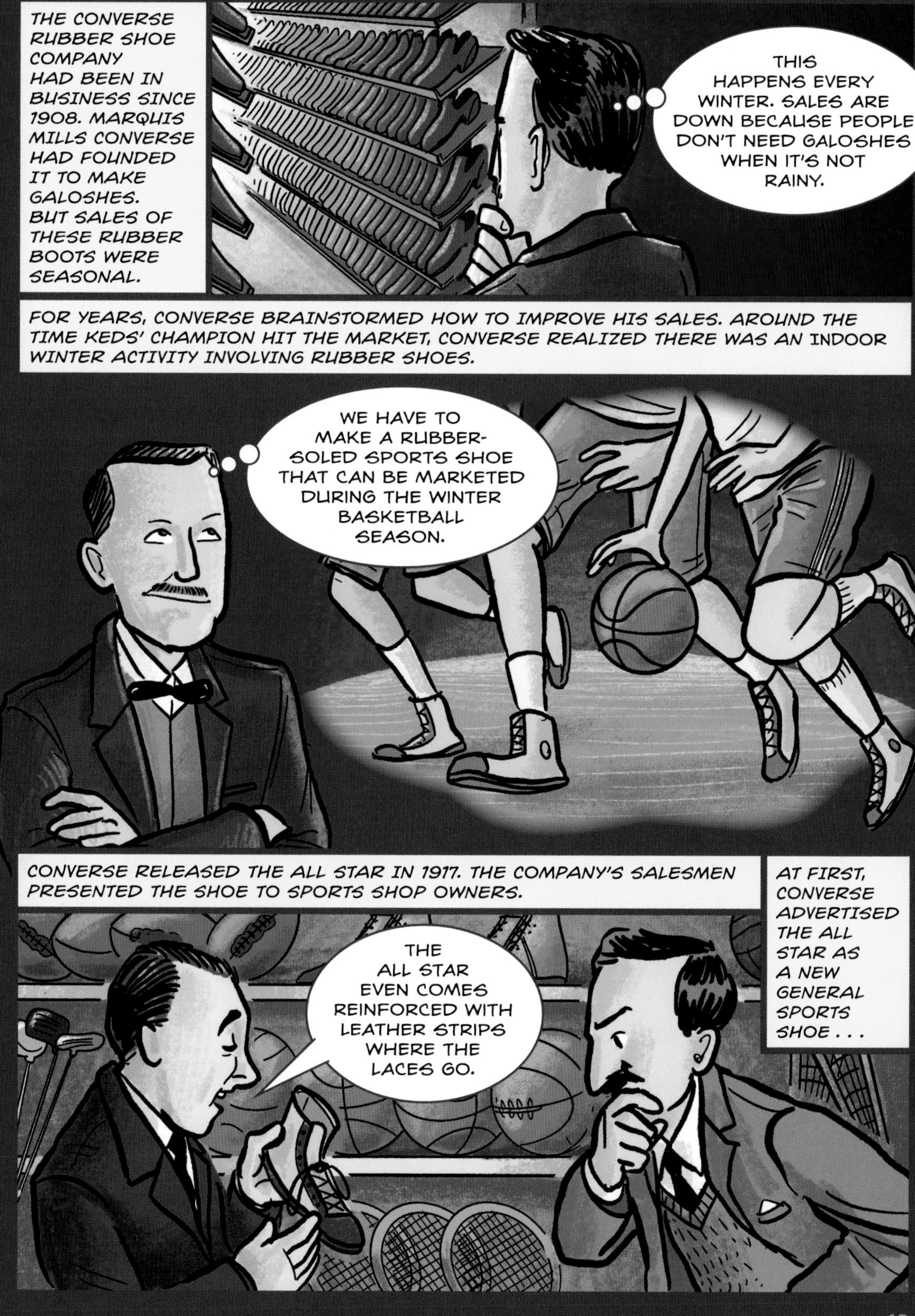
THE CONVERSE RUBBER SHOE COMPANY HAD BEEN IN BUSINESS SINCE 1908. MARQUIS MILLS CONVERSE HAD FOUNDED IT TO MAKE GALOSHES. BUT SALES OF THESE RUBBER BOOTS WERE SEASONAL.
THIS HAPPENS EVERY WINTER. SALES ARE DOWN BECAUSE PEOPLE DON'T NEED GALOSHES WHEN IT'S NOT RAINY.
FOR YEARS, CONVERSE BRAINSTORMED HOW TO IMPROVE HIS SALES. AROUND THE TIME KEDS' CHAMPION HIT THE MARKET, CONVERSE REALIZED THERE WAS AN INDOOR WINTER ACTIVITY INVOLVING RUBBER SHOES.
WE HAVE TO MAKE A RUBBER-SOLED SPORTS SHOE THAT CAN BE MARKETED DURING THE WINTER BASKETBALL SEASON.
CONVERSE RELEASED THE ALL STAR IN 1917. THE COMPANY'S SALESMEN PRESENTED THE SHOE TO SPORTS SHOP OWNERS.
AT FIRST, CONVERSE ADVERTISED THE ALL STAR AS A NEW GENERAL SPORTS SHOE . . .
THE ALL STAR EVEN COMES REINFORCED WITH LEATHER STRIPS WHERE THE LACES GO.

. . . BUT ALL STARS' NON-SKID RUBBER SOLES MADE THE SHOES PERFECT FOR BASKETBALL. CONVERSE ALSO HIRED BASKETBALL PLAYER CHUCK TAYLOR TO PROMOTE ITS NEW SHOES. IN 1922, TAYLOR BEGAN WORKING FOR CONVERSE AS A SALESMAN.

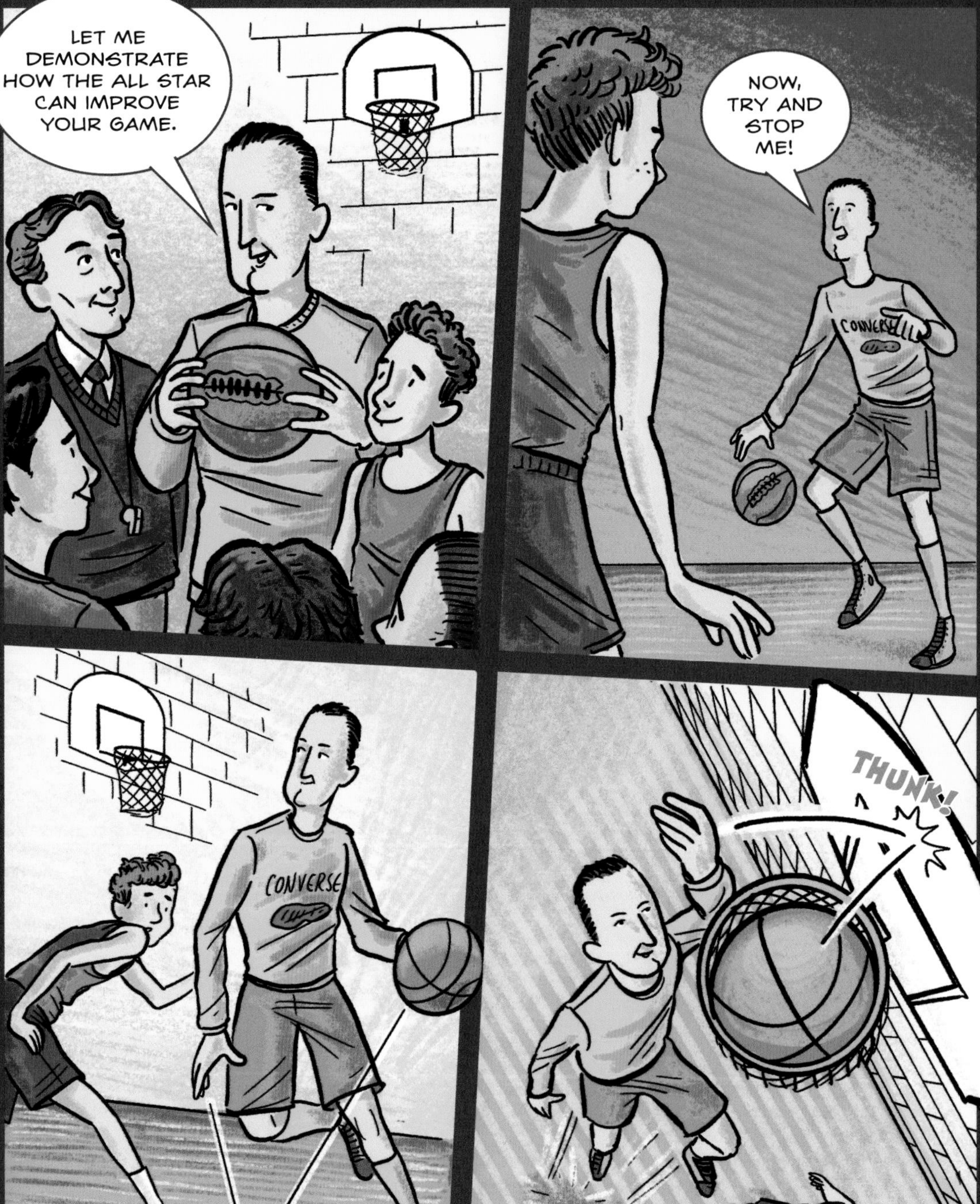
LET ME DEMONSTRATE HOW THE ALL STAR CAN IMPROVE YOUR GAME.
NOW, TRY AND STOP ME!
CONVERSE
CONVERSE
SQUEAK
SQUEAK
THUNK!

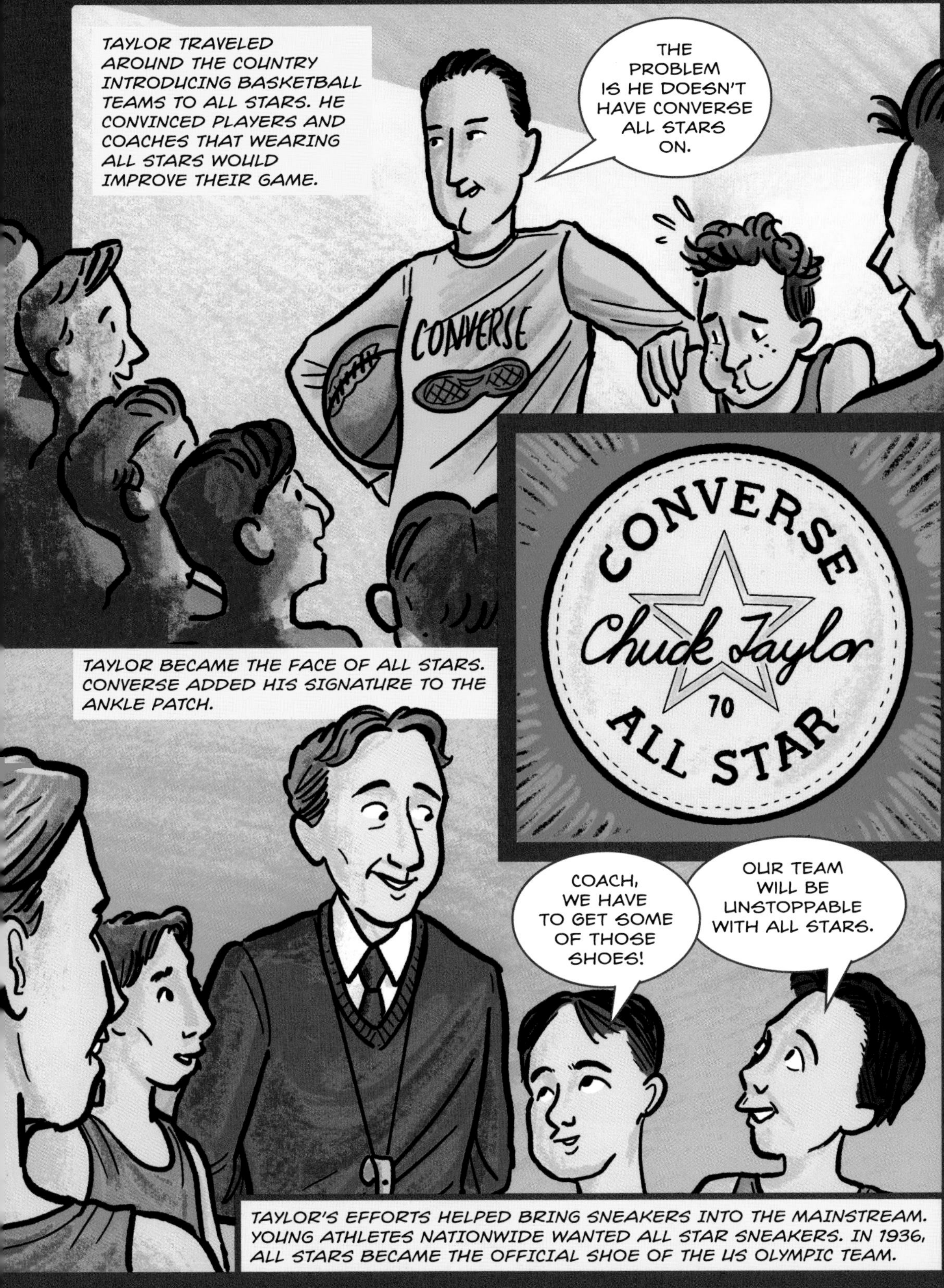
TAYLOR TRAVELED AROUND THE COUNTRY INTRODUCING BASKETBALL TEAMS TO ALL STARS. HE CONVINCED PLAYERS AND COACHES THAT WEARING ALL STARS WOULD IMPROVE THEIR GAME.
THE PROBLEM IS HE DOESN'T HAVE CONVERSE ALL STARS ON.
CONVERSE
CONVERSE Chuck Taylor 70 ALL STAR
TAYLOR BECAME THE FACE OF ALL STARS. CONVERSE ADDED HIS SIGNATURE TO THE ANKLE PATCH.
COACH, WE HAVE TO GET SOME OF THOSE SHOES!
OUR TEAM WILL BE UNSTOPPABLE WITH ALL STARS.
TAYLOR'S EFFORTS HELPED BRING SNEAKERS INTO THE MAINSTREAM. YOUNG ATHLETES NATIONWIDE WANTED ALL STAR SNEAKERS. IN 1936, ALL STARS BECAME THE OFFICIAL SHOE OF THE US OLYMPIC TEAM.

CHAPTER 3

SPORTS & SNEAKERS

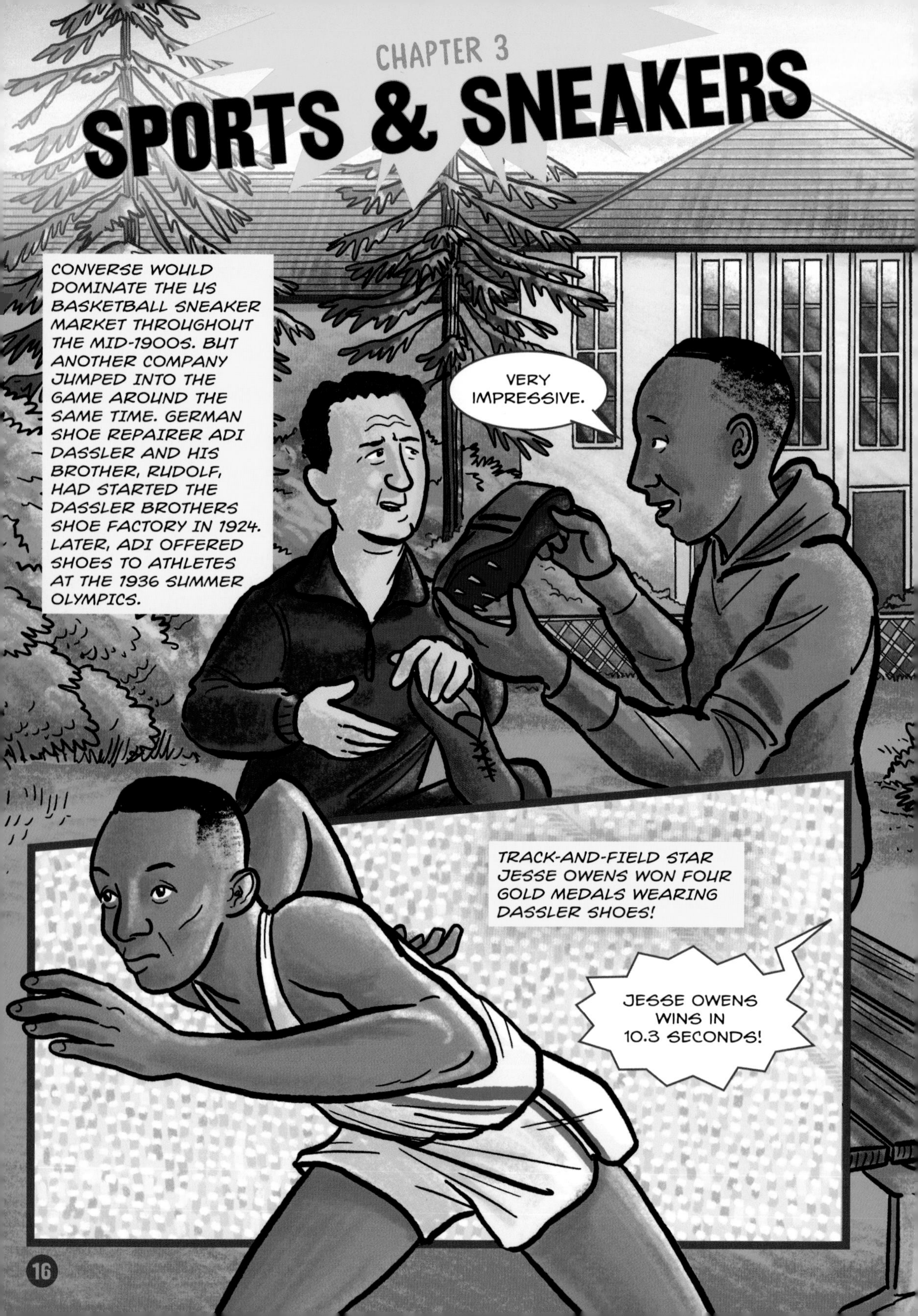
CONVERSE WOULD DOMINATE THE US BASKETBALL SNEAKER MARKET THROUGHOUT THE MID-1900S. BUT ANOTHER COMPANY JUMPED INTO THE GAME AROUND THE SAME TIME. GERMAN SHOE REPAIRER ADI DASSLER AND HIS BROTHER, RUDOLF, HAD STARTED THE DASSLER BROTHERS SHOE FACTORY IN 1924. LATER, ADI OFFERED SHOES TO ATHLETES AT THE 1936 SUMMER OLYMPICS.
VERY IMPRESSIVE.
TRACK-AND-FIELD STAR JESSE OWENS WON FOUR GOLD MEDALS WEARING DASSLER SHOES!
JESSE OWENS WINS IN 10.3 SECONDS!

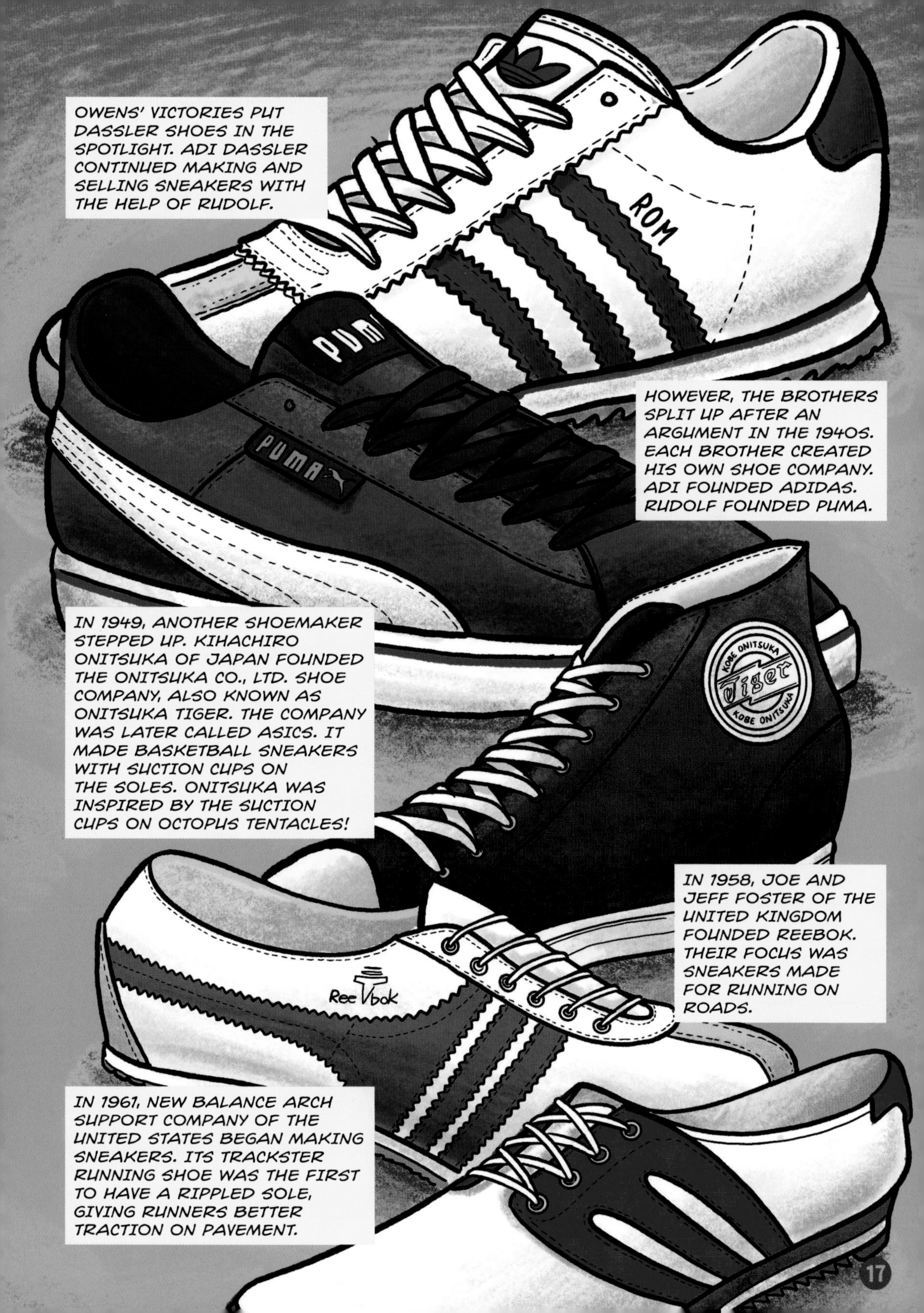
OWENS' VICTORIES PUT DASSLER SHOES IN THE SPOTLIGHT. ADI DASSLER CONTINUED MAKING AND SELLING SNEAKERS WITH THE HELP OF RUDOLF.
ROM
PUMA
HOWEVER, THE BROTHERS SPLIT UP AFTER AN ARGUMENT IN THE 1940S. EACH BROTHER CREATED HIS OWN SHOE COMPANY. ADI FOUNDED ADIDAS. RUDOLF FOUNDED PUMA.
PUMA
IN 1949, ANOTHER SHOEMAKER STEPPED UP. KIHACHIRO ONITSUKA OF JAPAN FOUNDED THE ONITSUKA CO., LTD. SHOE COMPANY, ALSO KNOWN AS ONITSUKA TIGER. THE COMPANY WAS LATER CALLED ASICS. IT MADE BASKETBALL SNEAKERS WITH SUCTION CUPS ON THE SOLES. ONITSUKA WAS INSPIRED BY THE SUCTION CUPS ON OCTOPUS TENTACLES!
KOBE ONITSUKA
Tiger
KOBE ONITSUKA
IN 1958, JOE AND JEFF FOSTER OF THE UNITED KINGDOM FOUNDED REEBOK. THEIR FOCUS WAS SNEAKERS MADE FOR RUNNING ON ROADS.
Reebok
IN 1961, NEW BALANCE ARCH SUPPORT COMPANY OF THE UNITED STATES BEGAN MAKING SNEAKERS. ITS TRACKSTER RUNNING SHOE WAS THE FIRST TO HAVE A RIPPLED SOLE, GIVING RUNNERS BETTER TRACTION ON PAVEMENT.

AS NEW SNEAKER COMPANIES CROPPED UP, ONE MAN FOCUSED ON COMPLETELY RETHINKING SNEAKERS. BILL BOWERMAN HAD BEEN THE TRACK-AND-FIELD COACH FOR THE UNIVERSITY OF OREGON SINCE 1949. FOR YEARS, HE WONDERED HOW ADVANCED EQUIPMENT COULD HELP HIS ATHLETES' PERFORMANCES.

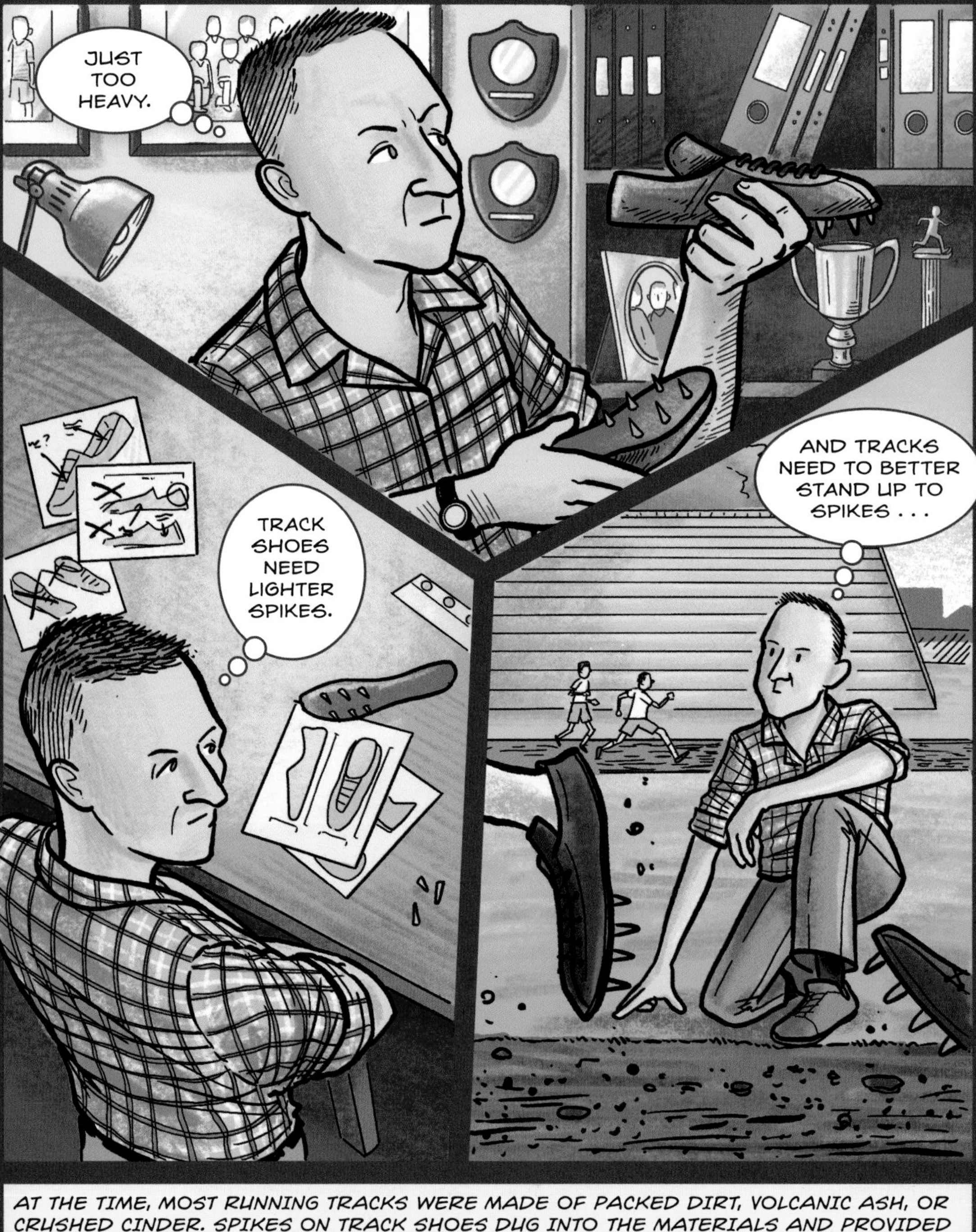
JUST TOO HEAVY.
TRACK SHOES NEED LIGHTER SPIKES.
AND TRACKS NEED TO BETTER STAND UP TO SPIKES . . .

AT THE TIME, MOST RUNNING TRACKS WERE MADE OF PACKED DIRT, VOLCANIC ASH, OR CRUSHED CINDER. SPIKES ON TRACK SHOES DUG INTO THE MATERIALS AND PROVIDED TRACTION, ESPECIALLY WHEN THE TRACK WAS WET. BUT THE SPIKES ALSO TORE CHUNKS OUT OF THE TRACK.

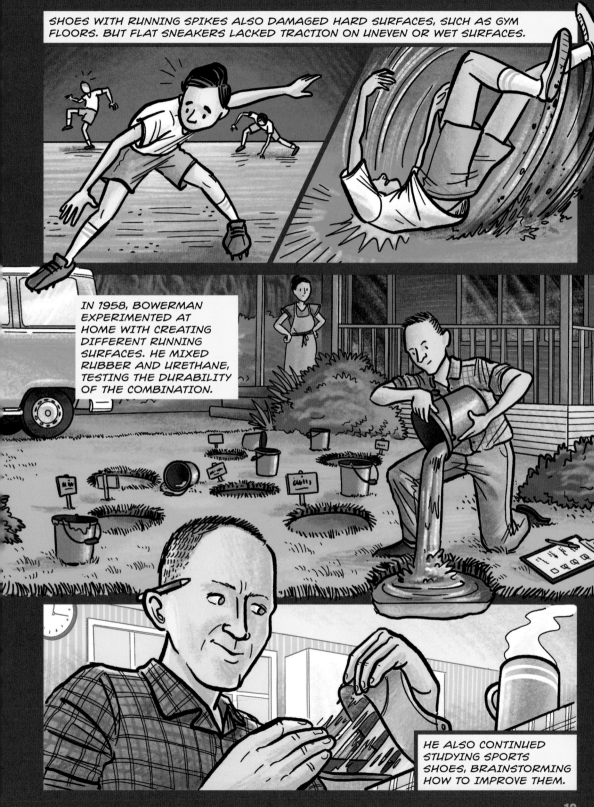

SHOES WITH RUNNING SPIKES ALSO DAMAGED HARD SURFACES, SUCH AS GYM FLOORS. BUT FLAT SNEAKERS LACKED TRACTION ON UNEVEN OR WET SURFACES.

IN 1958, BOWERMAN EXPERIMENTED AT HOME WITH CREATING DIFFERENT RUNNING SURFACES. HE MIXED RUBBER AND URETHANE, TESTING THE DURABILITY OF THE COMBINATION.

HE ALSO CONTINUED STUDYING SPORTS SHOES, BRAINSTORMING HOW TO IMPROVE THEM.

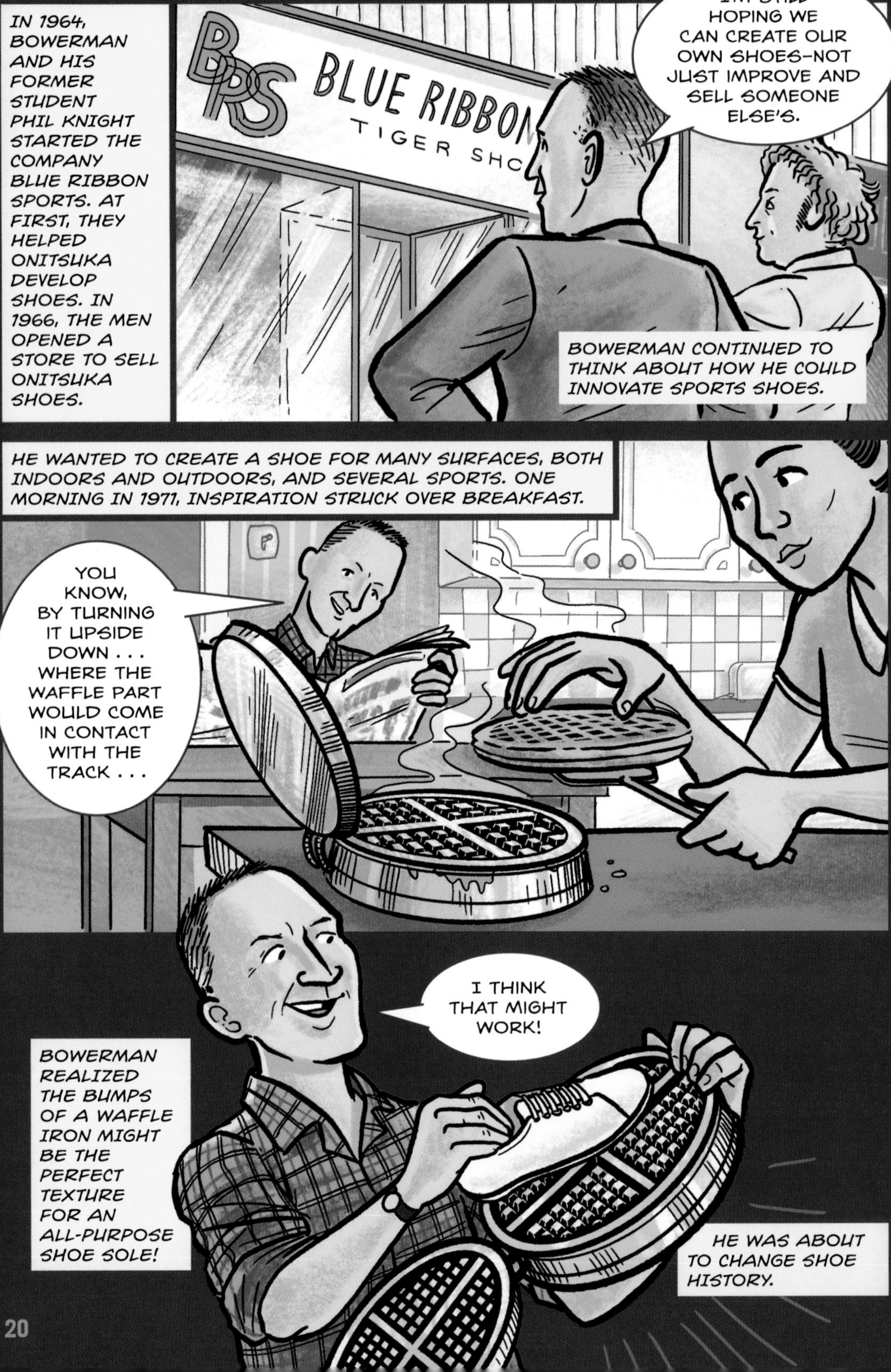
IN 1964, BOWERMAN AND HIS FORMER STUDENT PHIL KNIGHT STARTED THE COMPANY BLUE RIBBON SPORTS. AT FIRST, THEY HELPED ONITSUKA DEVELOP SHOES. IN 1966, THE MEN OPENED A STORE TO SELL ONITSUKA SHOES.
BRS
BLUE RIBBON
TIGER SHO
I'M STILL HOPING WE CAN CREATE OUR OWN SHOES—NOT JUST IMPROVE AND SELL SOMEONE ELSE'S.
BOWERMAN CONTINUED TO THINK ABOUT HOW HE COULD INNOVATE SPORTS SHOES.
HE WANTED TO CREATE A SHOE FOR MANY SURFACES, BOTH INDOORS AND OUTDOORS, AND SEVERAL SPORTS. ONE MORNING IN 1971, INSPIRATION STRUCK OVER BREAKFAST.
YOU KNOW, BY TURNING IT UPSIDE DOWN . . . WHERE THE WAFFLE PART WOULD COME IN CONTACT WITH THE TRACK . . .
I THINK THAT MIGHT WORK!
BOWERMAN REALIZED THE BUMPS OF A WAFFLE IRON MIGHT BE THE PERFECT TEXTURE FOR AN ALL-PURPOSE SHOE SOLE!
HE WAS ABOUT TO CHANGE SHOE HISTORY.

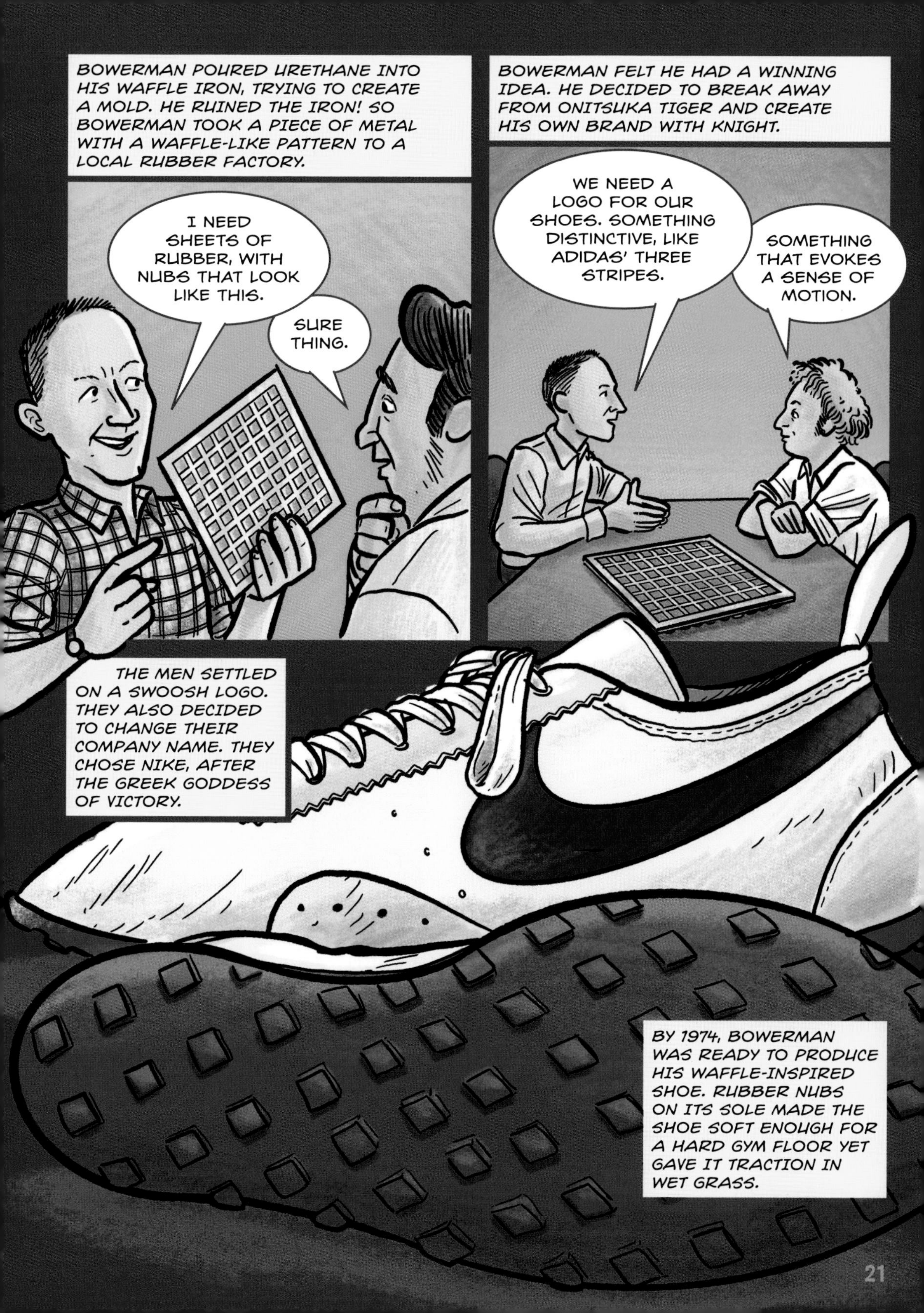
BOWERMAN POURED URETHANE INTO HIS WAFFLE IRON, TRYING TO CREATE A MOLD. HE RUINED THE IRON! SO BOWERMAN TOOK A PIECE OF METAL WITH A WAFFLE-LIKE PATTERN TO A LOCAL RUBBER FACTORY.
I NEED SHEETS OF RUBBER, WITH NUBS THAT LOOK LIKE THIS.
SURE THING.
BOWERMAN FELT HE HAD A WINNING IDEA. HE DECIDED TO BREAK AWAY FROM ONITSUKA TIGER AND CREATE HIS OWN BRAND WITH KNIGHT.
WE NEED A LOGO FOR OUR SHOES. SOMETHING DISTINCTIVE, LIKE ADIDAS' THREE STRIPES.
SOMETHING THAT EVOKES A SENSE OF MOTION.
THE MEN SETTLED ON A SWOOSH LOGO. THEY ALSO DECIDED TO CHANGE THEIR COMPANY NAME. THEY CHOSE NIKE, AFTER THE GREEK GODDESS OF VICTORY.
BY 1974, BOWERMAN WAS READY TO PRODUCE HIS WAFFLE-INSPIRED SHOE. RUBBER NUBS ON ITS SOLE MADE THE SHOE SOFT ENOUGH FOR A HARD GYM FLOOR YET GAVE IT TRACTION IN WET GRASS.

CHAPTER 4
FAME & FASHION

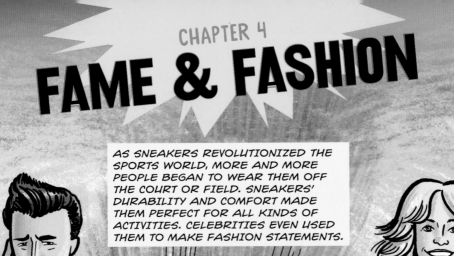

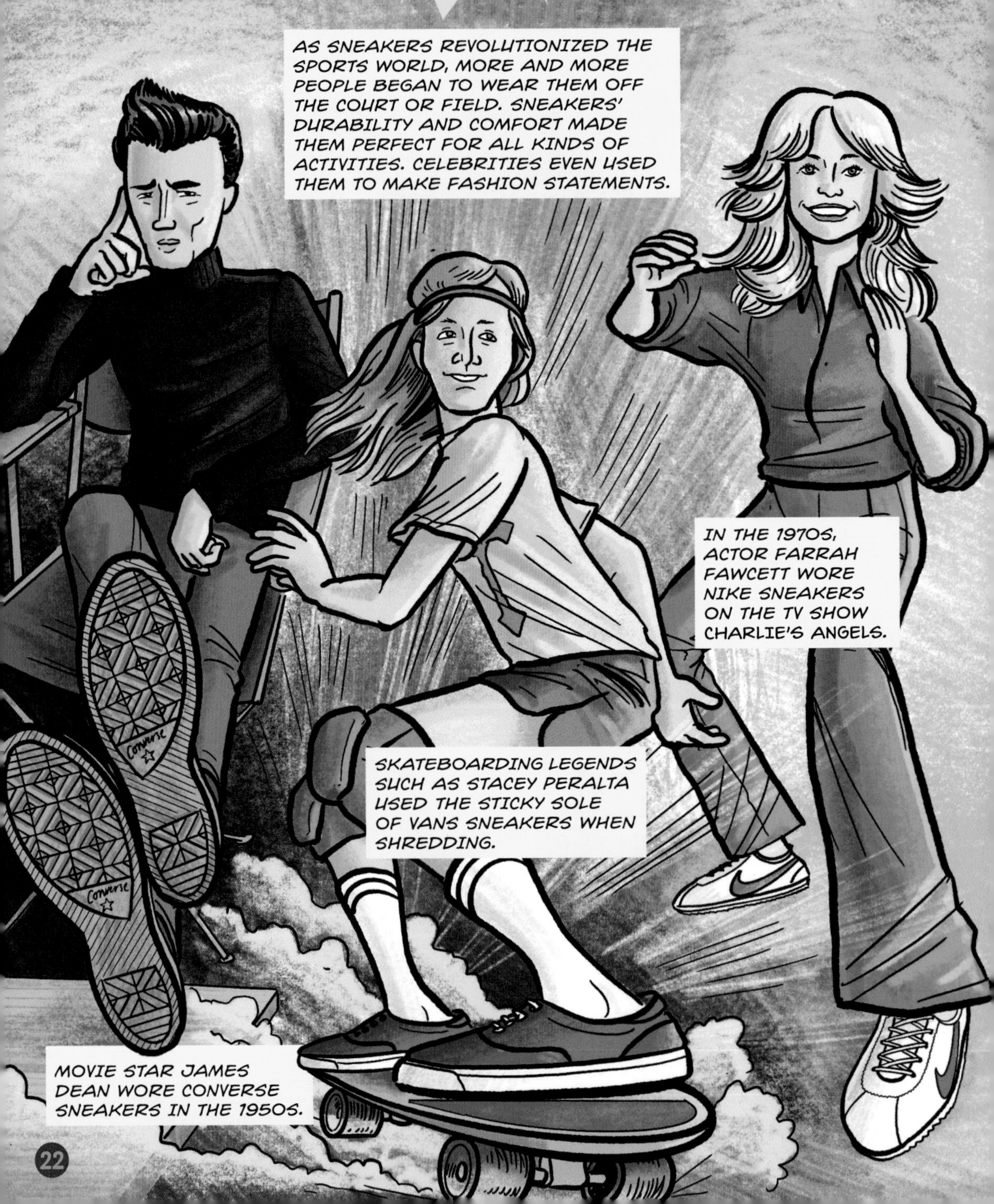
AS SNEAKERS REVOLUTIONIZED THE SPORTS WORLD, MORE AND MORE PEOPLE BEGAN TO WEAR THEM OFF THE COURT OR FIELD. SNEAKERS' DURABILITY AND COMFORT MADE THEM PERFECT FOR ALL KINDS OF ACTIVITIES. CELEBRITIES EVEN USED THEM TO MAKE FASHION STATEMENTS.
IN THE 1970S, ACTOR FARRAH FAWCETT WORE NIKE SNEAKERS ON THE TV SHOW CHARLIE'S ANGELS.
Converse
Converse
SKATEBOARDING LEGENDS SUCH AS STACEY PERALTA USED THE STICKY SOLE OF VANS SNEAKERS WHEN SHREDDING.
MOVIE STAR JAMES DEAN WORE CONVERSE SNEAKERS IN THE 1950S.

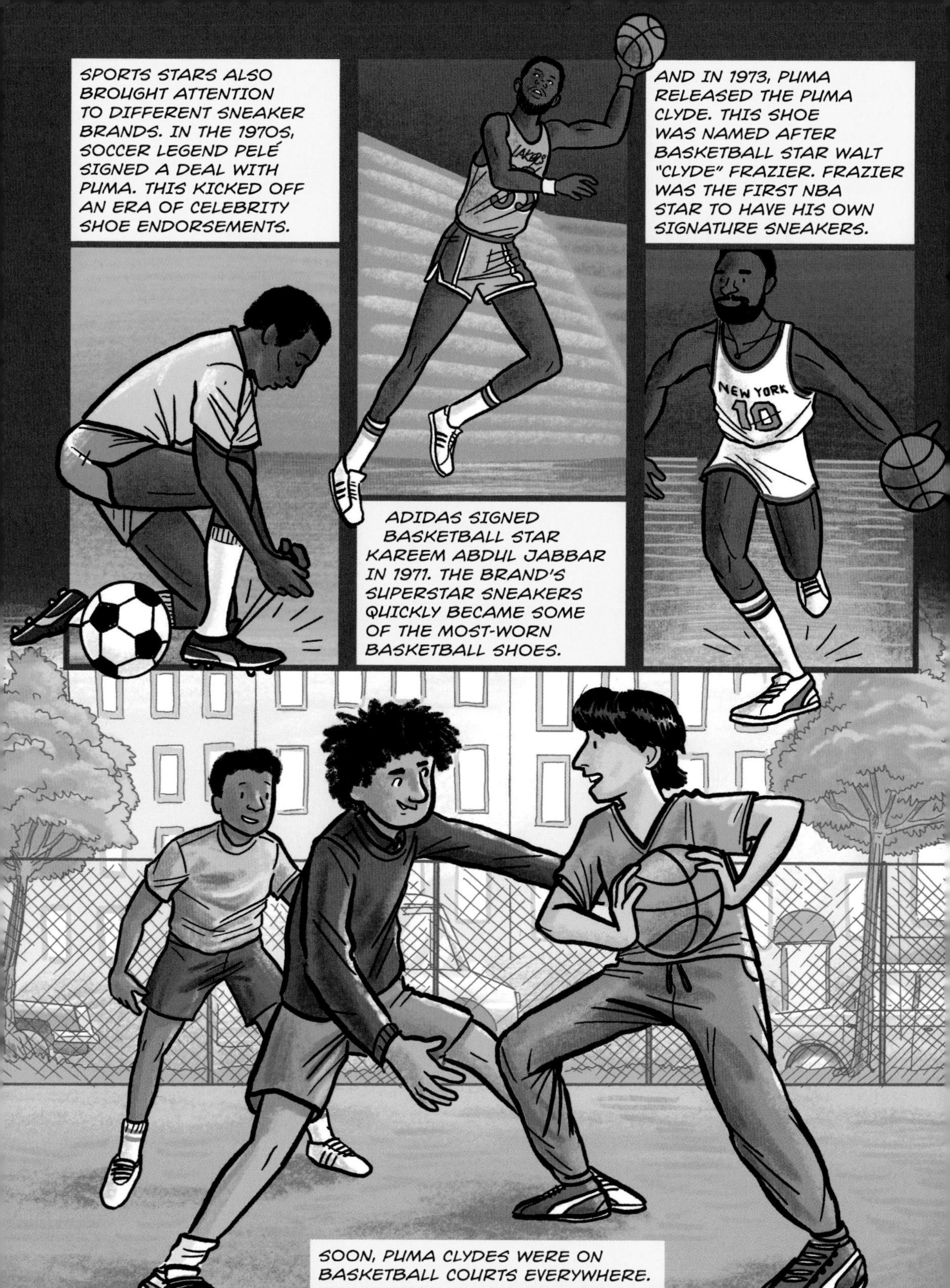
SPORTS STARS ALSO BROUGHT ATTENTION TO DIFFERENT SNEAKER BRANDS. IN THE 1970S, SOCCER LEGEND PELÉ SIGNED A DEAL WITH PUMA. THIS KICKED OFF AN ERA OF CELEBRITY SHOE ENDORSEMENTS.
LAKERS
ADIDAS SIGNED BASKETBALL STAR KAREEM ABDUL JABBAR IN 1971. THE BRAND'S SUPERSTAR SNEAKERS QUICKLY BECAME SOME OF THE MOST-WORN BASKETBALL SHOES.
AND IN 1973, PUMA RELEASED THE PUMA CLYDE. THIS SHOE WAS NAMED AFTER BASKETBALL STAR WALT "CLYDE" FRAZIER. FRAZIER WAS THE FIRST NBA STAR TO HAVE HIS OWN SIGNATURE SNEAKERS.
NEW YORK
10
SOON, PUMA CLYDES WERE ON BASKETBALL COURTS EVERYWHERE.

INTO THE 1980S, SOME CELEBRITIES, SUCH AS ACTOR JANE FONDA, LED A FITNESS CRAZE, STARRING IN AEROBICS VIDEOS FOR HOME USE.

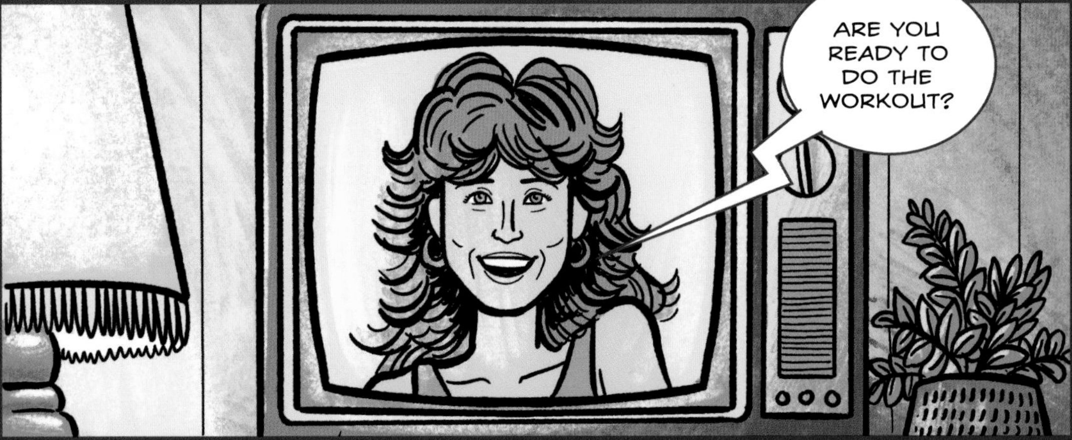
ARE YOU READY TO DO THE WORKOUT?

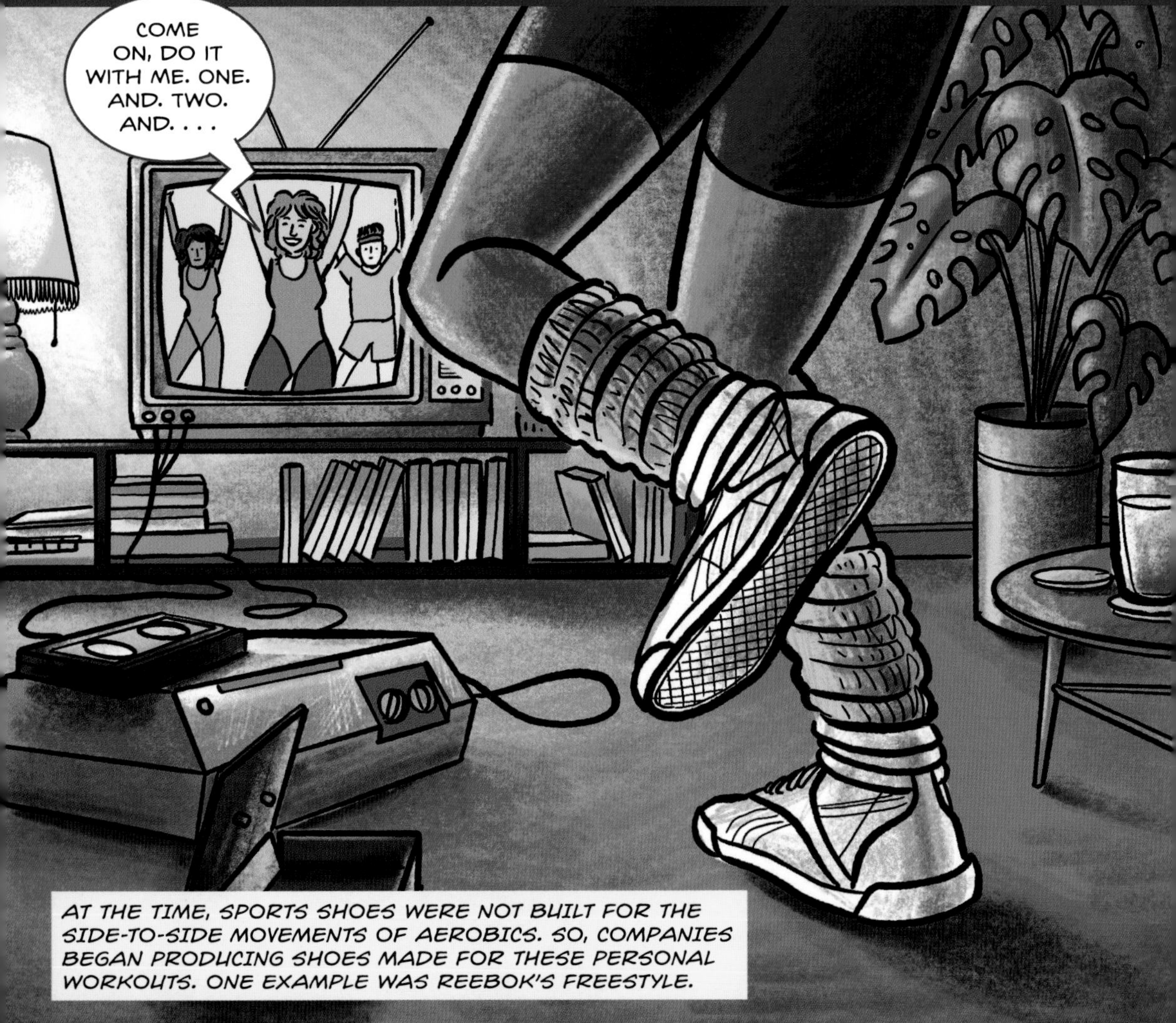
COME ON, DO IT WITH ME. ONE. AND. TWO. AND. . . .
AT THE TIME, SPORTS SHOES WERE NOT BUILT FOR THE SIDE-TO-SIDE MOVEMENTS OF AEROBICS. SO, COMPANIES BEGAN PRODUCING SHOES MADE FOR THESE PERSONAL WORKOUTS. ONE EXAMPLE WAS REEBOK'S FREESTYLE.

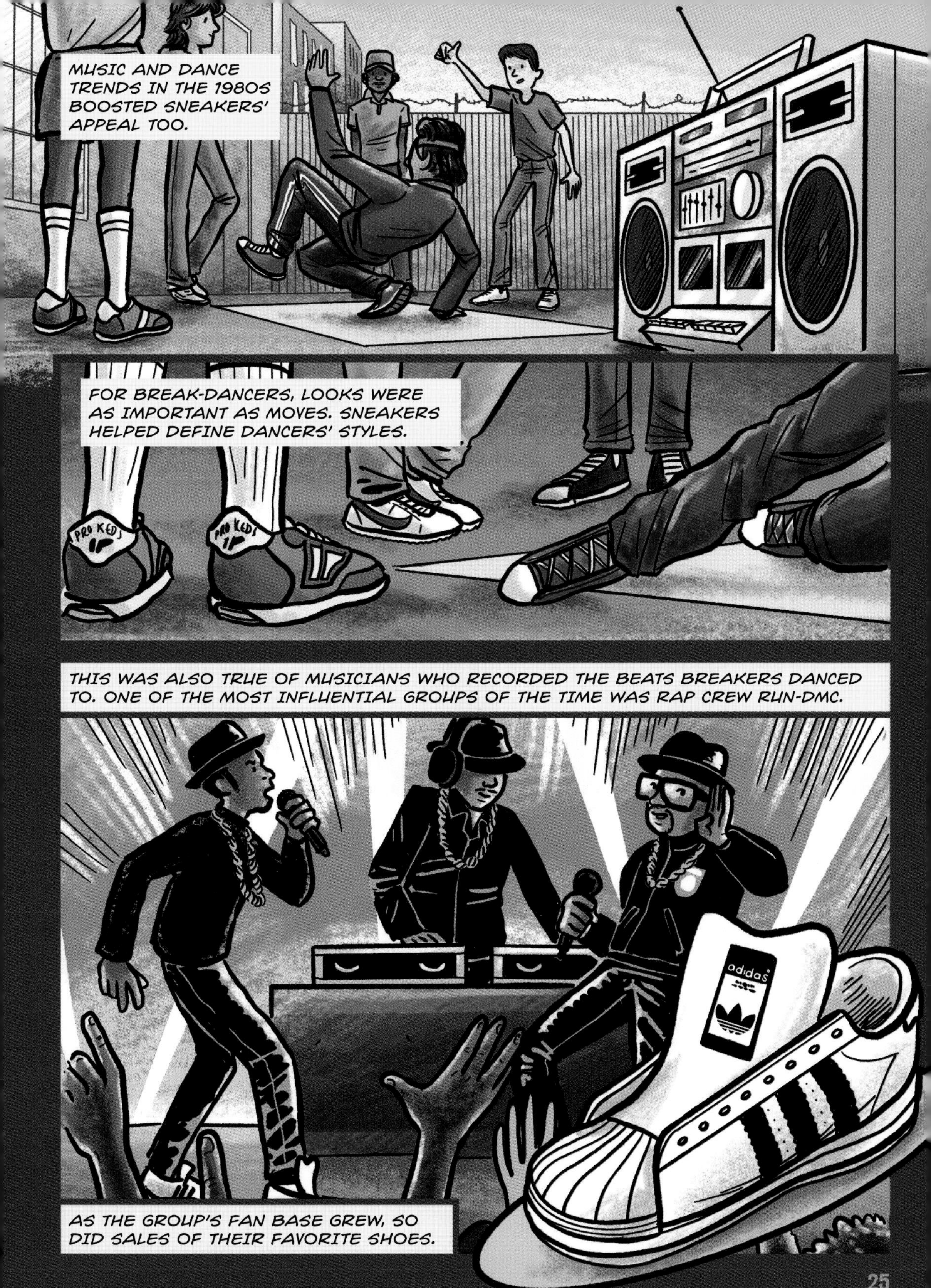
MUSIC AND DANCE TRENDS IN THE 1980S BOOSTED SNEAKERS' APPEAL TOO.
FOR BREAK-DANCERS, LOOKS WERE AS IMPORTANT AS MOVES. SNEAKERS HELPED DEFINE DANCERS' STYLES.
PRO KEDS
PRO KEDS
THIS WAS ALSO TRUE OF MUSICIANS WHO RECORDED THE BEATS BREAKERS DANCED TO. ONE OF THE MOST INFLUENTIAL GROUPS OF THE TIME WAS RAP CREW RUN-DMC.
adidas
AS THE GROUP'S FAN BASE GREW, SO DID SALES OF THEIR FAVORITE SHOES.

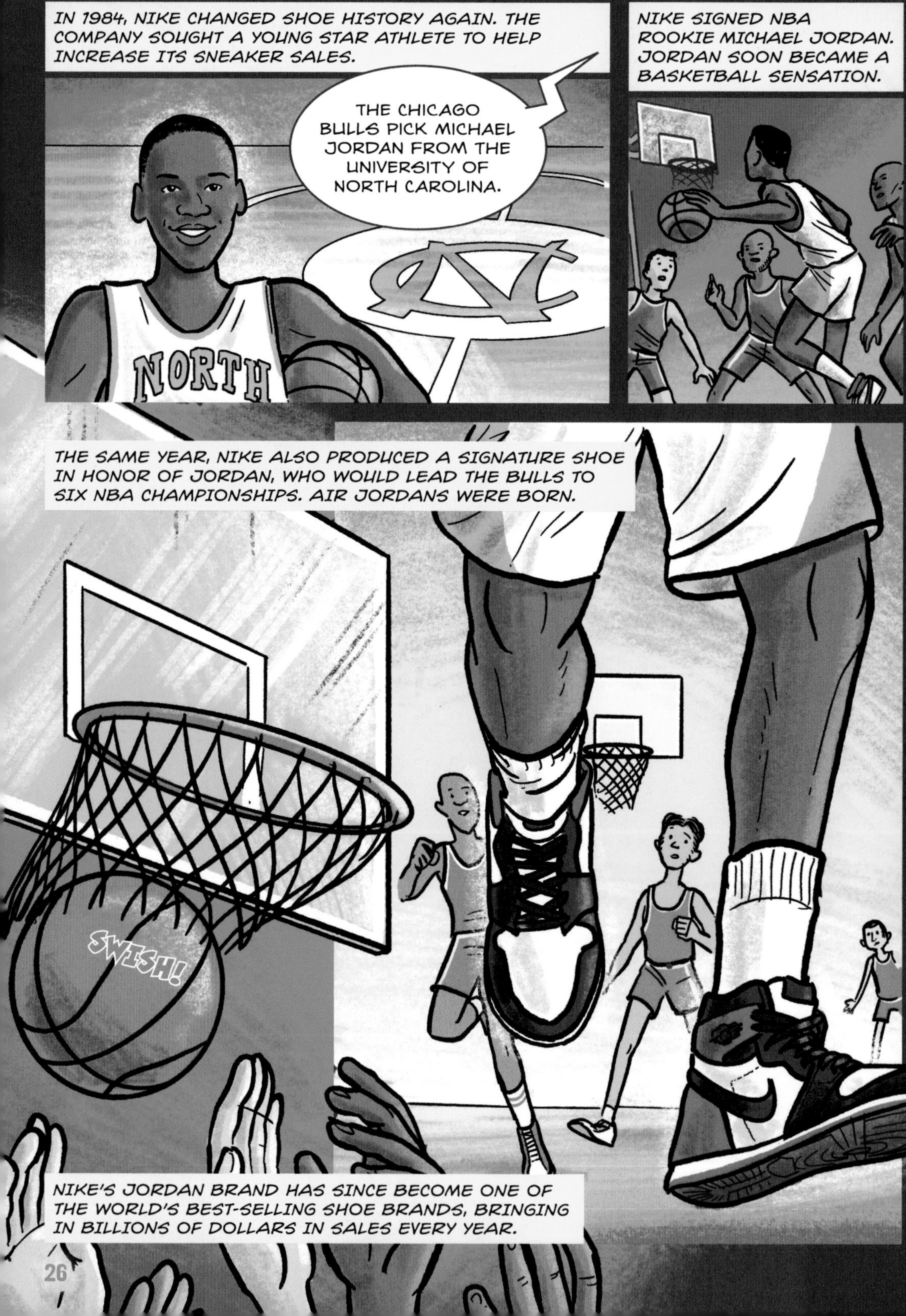
IN 1984, NIKE CHANGED SHOE HISTORY AGAIN. THE COMPANY SOUGHT A YOUNG STAR ATHLETE TO HELP INCREASE ITS SNEAKER SALES.
THE CHICAGO BULLS PICK MICHAEL JORDAN FROM THE UNIVERSITY OF NORTH CAROLINA.
NORTH
NIKE SIGNED NBA ROOKIE MICHAEL JORDAN. JORDAN SOON BECAME A BASKETBALL SENSATION.
THE SAME YEAR, NIKE ALSO PRODUCED A SIGNATURE SHOE IN HONOR OF JORDAN, WHO WOULD LEAD THE BULLS TO SIX NBA CHAMPIONSHIPS. AIR JORDANS WERE BORN.
SWISH!
NIKE'S JORDAN BRAND HAS SINCE BECOME ONE OF THE WORLD'S BEST-SELLING SHOE BRANDS, BRINGING IN BILLIONS OF DOLLARS IN SALES EVERY YEAR.

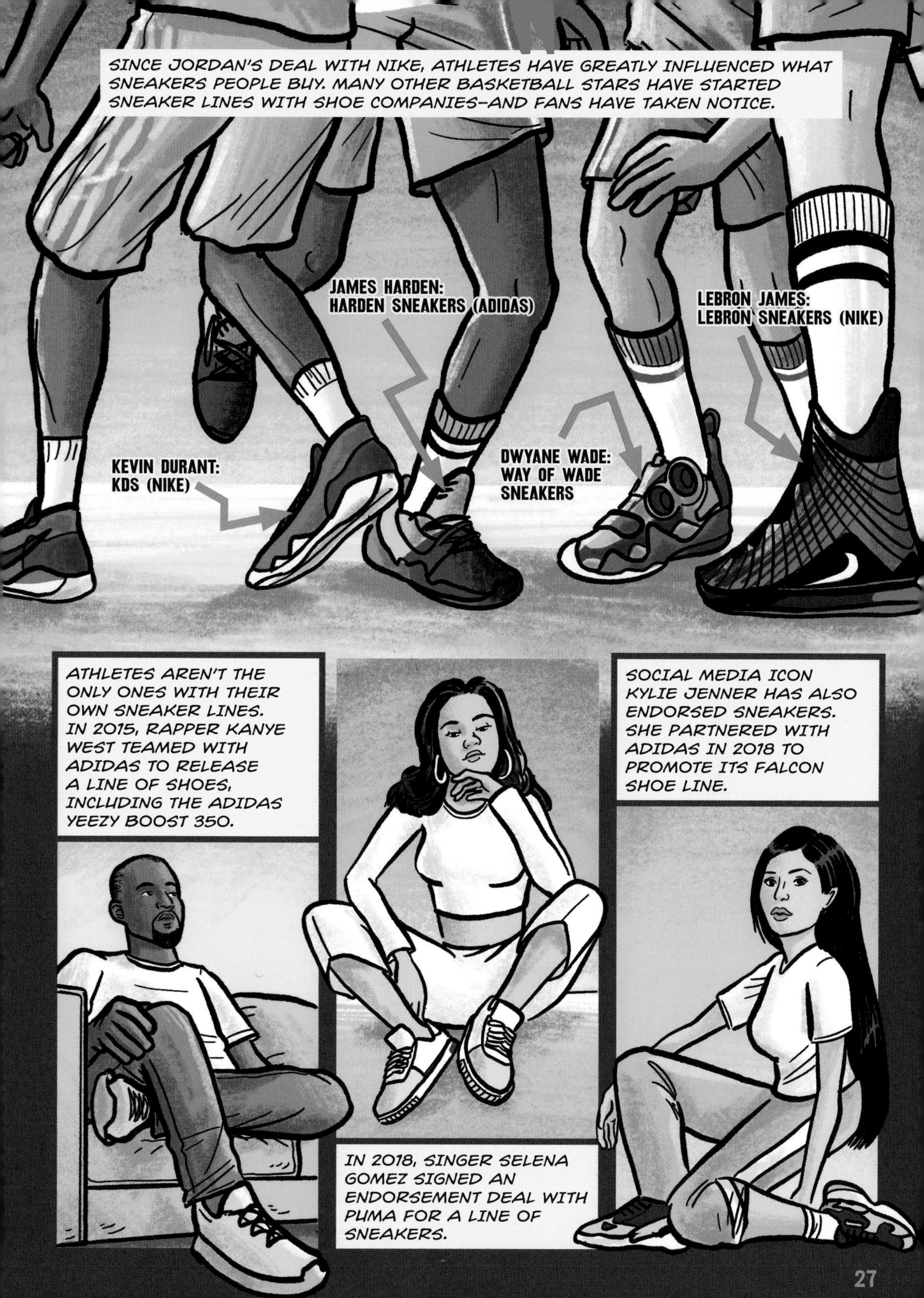
SINCE JORDAN'S DEAL WITH NIKE, ATHLETES HAVE GREATLY INFLUENCED WHAT SNEAKERS PEOPLE BUY. MANY OTHER BASKETBALL STARS HAVE STARTED SNEAKER LINES WITH SHOE COMPANIES—AND FANS HAVE TAKEN NOTICE.
JAMES HARDEN: HARDEN SNEAKERS (ADIDAS)
LEBRON JAMES: LEBRON SNEAKERS (NIKE)
KEVIN DURANT: KDS (NIKE)
DWYANE WADE: WAY OF WADE SNEAKERS
ATHLETES AREN'T THE ONLY ONES WITH THEIR OWN SNEAKER LINES. IN 2015, RAPPER KANYE WEST TEAMED WITH ADIDAS TO RELEASE A LINE OF SHOES, INCLUDING THE ADIDAS YEEZY BOOST 350.
IN 2018, SINGER SELENA GOMEZ SIGNED AN ENDORSEMENT DEAL WITH PUMA FOR A LINE OF SNEAKERS.
SOCIAL MEDIA ICON KYLIE JENNER HAS ALSO ENDORSED SNEAKERS. SHE PARTNERED WITH ADIDAS IN 2018 TO PROMOTE ITS FALCON SHOE LINE.

SNEAKERS HAVE BECOME THE MOST COMMON TYPE OF FOOTWEAR WORN BY PEOPLE WORLDWIDE. AND THEY CONTINUE TO EVOLVE.

SHOES IN THE NIKE ADAPT LINE DO NOT HAVE LACES. INSTEAD, A SMARTPHONE APP TIGHTENS THE "SELF-LACING" SHOES.

SOME COMPANIES ARE WORKING ON ENVIRONMENTALLY FRIENDLY SNEAKERS. VIVOBAREFOOT'S PRIMUS LITE II BIO SHOES ARE MADE FROM SUSTAINABLE PLANT-BASED MATERIALS.

PUMA CREATED LQD CELL ORIGIN AR SHOES FOR INTERACTIVE GAME PLAY. WHEN SEEN THROUGH A SMARTPHONE AUGMENTED REALITY APP, THE SHOES CAN LOOK AS THOUGH THEY ARE ON FIRE!

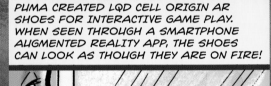

OTHER FUTURE SNEAKERS MIGHT GENERATE ELECTRICITY AS YOU WALK. AND, YOU MIGHT BE ABLE TO CHANGE A SNEAKER'S COLOR WITH AN APP. WHAT ELSE MIGHT SNEAKERS OF THE FUTURE DO? THE POSSIBILITIES ARE LIMITLESS!

SOURCE NOTES

PAGE 15

Nicholas Smith, *Kicks: The Great American Story of Sneakers* (New York: Crown Publishing Group, 2018) 45.

PAGES 20–21

"Nike's Holy Grail: Bowerman Family Unearths Long-Lost Waffle Iron," OregonLive, The Oregonian, Jan 10, 2019, https://www.oregonlive.com/behindducksbeat/2011/02/nikes_holy_grail_bowerman_fami.html.

PAGE 21

Nicholas Smith, *Kicks: The Great American Story of Sneakers* (New York: Crown Publishing Group, 2018) 104.

PAGE 24

"1970s: Jane Fonda Workout," YouTube video, 00:01, Mar 21, 2018, https://www.youtube.com/watch?v=u86NaR3z6FE.

PAGE 26

"The Chicago Bulls pick MICHAEL JORDAN! Draft Video," YouTube video, 00:01, Jul 19, 2007, https://www.youtube.com/watch?v=0B9obsY_Yg8.

GLOSSARY

ARCH SUPPORT: rigid molding built into or placed inside a shoe to support a foot's arch

AUGMENTED REALITY: technology that places a digital overlay of imagery on top of real imagery being viewed through a device such as a smartphone or tablet

DURABLE: able to withstand wear and tear

PATENT: an official document that protects its owner's rights to an invention. To apply for and receive this document is to patent.

SULFUR: a yellow, nonmetallic chemical that is a solid at room temperature

TRACTION: the force that keeps a moving body from slipping on a surface

UPPER: the part of a shoe that covers the toes, top, and sides of the foot

VELCRO: a fastener made of two strips of nylon fabric, one with tiny hooks and the other with a clinging material

VULCANIZE: to harden rubber by treating it with sulfur

LEARN MORE

Goodyear—The Charles Goodyear Story
https://corporate.goodyear.com/en-US/about
/history/charles-goodyear-story.html

Jozefowicz, Chris. *10 Fascinating Facts about
Sneakers*. New York: Children's Press, 2017.

Kansas Historical Society—James Naismith
https://www.kshs.org/kansapedia/james-naismith/12154

Keyser, Amber. *Sneaker Century: A History of Athletic Shoes*.
Minneapolis: Twenty-First Century Books, 2015.

Nike—Bill Bowerman
https://purpose.nike.com/bill-bowerman

Smithsonian Institution—A Brief History of America's Obsession with Sneakers
https://www.smithsonianmag.com/innovation/brief-history-americas-obsession
-sneakers-180969116/

INDEX